AF422427

# Two Bodies & One Soul

Two Bodies & One Soul
Copyright © [2025] by Pradeep K. Berry
All rights reserved.

No part of this publication may be reproduced, distributed, or transmitted in any form or by any means, including photocopying, recording, or other electronic or mechanical methods, without the prior written permission of the publisher, except in the case of brief quotations embodied in critical reviews and certain other noncommercial uses permitted by copyright law.

This is a work of fiction. Names, characters, places, and incidents either are the product of the author's imagination or are used fictitiously. Any resemblance to actual persons, living or dead, events, or locales is entirely coincidental.

# Dedication

To Connie, my beloved wife, my soulmate, the other half of my soul. This book, a testament to our forty-one years together, is a tribute to the depth of our love, a love that transcended the physical realm and continues to resonate in the quiet spaces of my heart. It is a journey through grief, a struggle for justice, and a testament to the enduring power of a bond so profound it defied the boundaries of life and death. This is for you, my Connie, forever and always. My love, my life, my everything. May this imperfect offering serve as a small echo of the immeasurable joy and unwavering love you brought to my life. For your enduring spirit, your unwavering grace, and your boundless love, this work is dedicated to you, the woman who taught me the true meaning of life, and showed me how to find light even in the darkest of nights. Your memory continues to illuminate my path, guiding me through the labyrinth of loss and toward a future shaped by your love and legacy. I love you, eternally.

# Preface

Writing this book has been a cathartic, agonizing, and ultimately, necessary process. The loss of Connie, my wife of forty-one years, left a chasm in my life, a void that seemed impossible to fill. Her death, shrouded in the complications of alleged medical negligence, further intensified the pain, fueling a righteous anger that spurred me to seek justice. This memoir is not merely a recounting of our life together; it is a journey through the darkest corners of grief, an exploration of philosophical and spiritual perspectives that offered solace, and a chronicle of my fight for accountability. Through the lens of my experience, I aim to shed light on the complexities of grief, the frustrating realities of medical malpractice, and the enduring power of love in the face of immense loss. My hope is that this narrative will resonate with those who have traversed similar paths, offering comfort, understanding, and a sense of shared experience. It is also my hope that it might inspire others to seek justice when faced with injustice, and to find strength in the face of adversity. The wisdom gleaned from the teachings of Lord Krishna and Chanakya, interwoven throughout the narrative, provides a framework for understanding loss, accepting the inevitability of death, and finding meaning in the face of suffering. This is a deeply personal account, yet I believe its themes are universal, transcending the particularities of my experience to touch upon the shared human experience of love, loss, and the enduring search for meaning.

# Introduction

Forty-one years. Forty-one years of shared laughter, whispered secrets, and a love so profound it felt preordained, a destiny woven into the very fabric of our being – two bodies, one soul. This is the story of that love, a love that blossomed from an initial meeting and bloomed through decades of shared experiences, mutual growth, and unwavering commitment. It is the story of Connie and me, a narrative that encompasses joy and triumph, but is ultimately defined by the agonizing loss that shattered my world in 2015. This book delves into the depths of my grief, a grief so profound it threatened to consume me. It explores the emotional turmoil of witnessing Connie's battle with cancer, the trauma of her death, and the subsequent struggle to navigate a life without her. However, it is not solely a lament. It is also a testament to the strength of the human spirit, to the resilience of love, and to the possibility of finding meaning even in the face of unimaginable pain. Through personal anecdotes, philosophical reflections, and spiritual insights, I aim to illuminate the complexities of loss, the importance of justice, and the enduring power of human connection. The alleged medical negligence that contributed to Connie's death fuels a significant portion of this narrative, shaping my determination to seek accountability and to advocate for systemic change within the healthcare system. My journey through grief has been interwoven with a deeper exploration of spiritual and philosophical concepts, drawing on the wisdom of ancient teachers like Lord Krishna and Chanakya, whose teachings on acceptance, duty, and the search for meaning have provided solace and guidance. This memoir, then, is a testament not only to the love I shared with Connie but also to the profound lessons learned during the most challenging period of my life. It is a journey of loss, of anger, of healing, and ultimately, of hope.

## The Genesis of Our Bond

It began, as many transformative moments do, unexpectedly. I hadn't been actively searching for a wife; life, as it often does, had other plans. I met Connie at a conference on international relations – a field we both deeply cared about, although our approaches differed. She was a whirlwind of energy, articulate and sharp-witted, possessing a profound intellect that immediately captivated me. Her laughter, a melodic cascade, echoed in the halls long after our initial conversation. I, a typically reserved academic, found myself completely disarmed by her vibrant spirit. There was an immediate connection, a shared understanding that transcended the polite formalities of the event. We talked for hours that day, discussing everything from the intricacies of geopolitical strategy to our shared love for classical music and the absurdities of everyday life. It felt as if we had known each other for lifetimes.

Our early courtship was a vibrant tapestry woven with shared experiences. We devoured books together, discussing philosophical treatises late into the night, our arguments often as passionate and engaging as our agreements. We explored the hidden corners of our city, discovering quaint cafes and forgotten parks, creating a personal mythology of our burgeoning relationship. There was a depth to our conversations, a willingness to be vulnerable and honest with each other that established a foundation of trust and intimacy that would endure for over four decades. We found a kindred spirit in one another – a rarity I now understand to be precious beyond measure.

The values we shared were not simply superficial agreements; they formed the bedrock of our commitment.

We both possessed a deep-seated commitment to social justice, a belief in the power of education, and a profound respect for different cultures and perspectives. These weren't merely topics of discussion; they were guiding principles that shaped our daily lives. We volunteered at local charities, participated in political campaigns, and travelled extensively, broadening our understanding of the world and enriching our lives immeasurably. This shared ethical compass, this commitment to a life lived with meaning and purpose, became the invisible glue that held our relationship together through times of both joy and profound sorrow.

Our marriage, celebrated in a small ceremony surrounded by close family and friends, felt less like a legal contract and more like a sacred covenant. It wasn't a fairytale; we had our disagreements, our moments of frustration and misunderstanding. But underlying these inevitable bumps in the road was an unwavering respect for each other's individuality, a deep understanding of our shared dreams, and a commitment to work through challenges together. We approached our marriage not as a passive acceptance of fate, but as a dynamic partnership requiring constant nurturing and communication. This meant embracing each other's flaws and celebrating each other's triumphs, acknowledging that a truly successful marriage was not about perfection, but about perseverance and a mutual desire for growth.

Those early years were a whirlwind of discovery and shared adventures. We moved to a new city together, embracing the challenges and excitement of building a life from scratch. We both pursued our careers with passion and dedication, supporting each other's aspirations without reservation. Our shared love of travel took us to far-flung corners of the globe, from the bustling markets of Marrakech to the serene temples of Kyoto. Each journey was not just a sightseeing expedition; it was an opportunity to learn, to grow, and to deepen our understanding of ourselves and the world around us. These experiences, documented in photos and journals, are not mere snapshots of our past, but vivid reminders of the depth of our connection.

The intellectual stimulation we provided each other was as vital as the physical intimacy. We devoured books, attended lectures and performances, and engaged in lively debates that stretched late into the night. Our home was a haven for stimulating conversation, a place where ideas flowed freely and where we challenged each other to think critically and creatively. We even collaborated on several projects – academic papers, articles, and creative writing endeavors. The process of working together, bouncing ideas off each other, and critiquing each other's work solidified our partnership in a unique way. These collaborative efforts were not merely professional achievements; they were tangible manifestations of our mutual respect and unwavering support.

As the years progressed, we added new chapters to our story: the arrival of children, the joys and challenges of parenthood, the fulfillment of career goals, and the bittersweet experience of watching our children embark on their own journeys. Each milestone, each triumph and each setback, strengthened the bond between us. We faced financial hardships and professional setbacks together, learning to navigate adversity with grace and resilience. It was during these challenging times that the true strength of our commitment became evident. We learned to lean on each other, to offer support and encouragement when words failed, and to find solace in our shared love and unwavering belief in one another. The years were not always easy, yet we faced every storm as one unit, a testament to the powerful foundation we had established early in our relationship.

Looking back, I recognize that our connection was more profound than simply a deep love or shared values. There was a sense of destiny, of a preordained connection that transcended the ordinary. It was a feeling of having found my soulmate, my other half. We were indeed, as I would later write in the title of this book, "two bodies and one soul." The philosophy of 'two bodies and one soul' wasn't merely a romantic notion; it was a lived reality. It was a shared consciousness, a mutual understanding that went beyond words or explanations. It was a sense of completion, of finding my mirror image in Connie, someone who understood me completely, flaws and all. This profound connection formed the unwavering anchor that sustained us through every challenge and heartbreak we faced. It is this connection, this shared soul, that continues to sustain me even in the face of my unimaginable loss. The pain is acute, the absence unbearable, yet the memory of our shared life, our two bodies and one soul, provides a flickering beacon of hope amidst the darkness.

## Shared Dreams and Aspirations

Our shared passions weren't merely hobbies; they were the vibrant threads that wove the tapestry of our life together. Travel, for instance, wasn't just about ticking off destinations on a list; it was about immersing ourselves in different cultures, tasting unfamiliar cuisines, and absorbing the unique beauty of each place. We journeyed across Europe, from the bustling streets of Rome to the serene canals of Venice, our conversations as lively and engaging as the sights around us. We explored the ancient ruins of Greece, marveling at the architectural prowess of civilizations long past, our discussions often veering into philosophical debates about the nature of time and mortality. These weren't simply tourist trips; they were adventures into shared understanding, deepening our connection with each other and the world around us. The shared experience of witnessing the ethereal beauty of the Northern Lights in Iceland, the humbling vastness of the Grand Canyon, or the vibrant energy of a bustling Marrakech souk, solidified our bond, creating memories etched not just in photographs, but in the very fabric of our being. These weren't just moments; they were milestones in our shared journey.

Our love for the arts manifested in countless ways. We attended countless concerts, operas, and theatre performances, often engaging in passionate discussions about the nuances of the performances afterwards, dissecting the directorial choices, the actor's portrayals, and the composer's intentions. We spent countless hours in museums, absorbing the masterpieces of renowned artists, our conversations weaving together art history, philosophy, and personal interpretations. We weren't passive observers; we were active participants in the creative process, our own lives enriched by the beauty we experienced. We collected art ourselves – not for investment, but for the joy it brought us, each piece a silent testament to a shared aesthetic sensibility, a shared moment of appreciation and understanding. We even dabbled in creating art ourselves; Connie, with her innate talent, took up painting, her canvases blossoming with vibrant colours and expressive strokes. I, in my more measured approach, found solace in photography, capturing moments of beauty and capturing the essence of our shared experiences. Our home was a reflection of this shared passion, a gallery of our lives, our journey, our shared appreciation for beauty in all its forms.

But perhaps our most significant shared passion was our commitment to intellectual pursuits. We both thrived on stimulating conversations, engaging in debates that spanned a wide spectrum of topics – from the intricacies of international politics and economics to the complexities of human psychology and philosophy. We devoured books together, often engaging in lengthy discussions about the ideas and perspectives presented. Our home was filled with books, overflowing bookshelves a testament to our shared love for knowledge and learning. We attended lectures and seminars together, challenging each other's perspectives and expanding our understanding of the world. Our intellectual curiosity was insatiable, our thirst for knowledge a shared flame that burned brightly throughout our lives. This shared intellectual journey was more than just a pursuit of knowledge; it was a partnership in discovery, a shared quest for wisdom and understanding. We learned from each other, challenged each other, and inspired each other to reach beyond our limitations.

Connie's sharp intellect and analytical mind were a constant source of inspiration to me. She possessed a keen ability to dissect complex issues, identifying the underlying patterns and connections that often escaped me. Her insights often provided a fresh perspective, challenging my assumptions and forcing me to reconsider my own positions. We often spent hours discussing international affairs, engaging in debates that were both rigorous and passionate. Her understanding of political dynamics and strategic thinking was remarkable, offering a counterpoint to my own more theoretical approach. These intellectual exchanges were not just arguments; they were explorations of ideas, a collaborative process of expanding our understanding. This constant exchange of ideas fuelled our shared journey, propelling us forward in our individual pursuits and enriching our relationship. Her insights informed my academic work, enriching my research and broadening my perspective. Her contributions were essential to my academic success. Her loss, therefore, is not just a personal tragedy, but a professional one as well.

Our shared commitment to intellectual exploration extended beyond academic pursuits. We were avid learners, always seeking to expand our horizons and deepen our understanding of the world. We attended workshops, took online courses, and engaged in self-directed learning, pursuing topics that piqued our interest. We were not afraid to embrace new challenges, always striving to learn something new and push our intellectual boundaries. This lifelong commitment to learning was deeply intertwined with our spirituality. We were fascinated by diverse philosophical traditions, exploring the wisdom of ancient cultures and drawing parallels between seemingly disparate belief systems. We found solace and inspiration in spiritual texts, studying the teachings of figures like Lord Krishna and Chanakya, reflecting on their insights about life, death, and the human condition. These studies provided a framework for understanding our experiences, giving meaning to our shared journey and providing a source of comfort and strength during times of adversity. This shared exploration of spiritual and philosophical concepts provided a deeper context to our lives, giving us a framework through which to navigate both joy and sorrow.

Our shared love of travel, art, and intellectual pursuits wasn't just about personal fulfillment; it was a testament to our shared values. We believed in the importance of continuous learning, of expanding our horizons, and of engaging with the world around us. These shared passions weren't simply activities; they were the foundation upon which we built our lives together, the mortar that held the bricks of our shared existence firmly in place. They were not merely hobbies or interests; they were the very essence of our relationship, a tangible representation of our 'two bodies and one soul.' These experiences weren't merely memories; they were the building blocks of our shared identity, a testament to the profound depth and enduring nature of our love. They were a constant source of joy, companionship, and mutual growth – an unending source of comfort, even now, in the face of overwhelming loss. The vibrant colors of our shared experiences still paint my memories, even as the acute pain of her absence persists. And in these memories, I find not only solace, but a renewed determination to honor the life we built together, a life woven together from the threads of shared dreams and aspirations. The tapestry, though incomplete, still holds a profound and enduring beauty. The pattern remains, even in its incompletion, reminding me of the profound bond we shared, a bond that, even in death, continues to shape my life. This is the legacy Connie leaves behind, a living testament to our 'two bodies and one soul.' The profound imprint of our shared life continues to resonate within me, providing a guiding light through the darkness of grief.

## Building a Life of Shared Purpose

Our shared passions extended beyond leisure; they were the bedrock upon which we built a life of shared purpose. It wasn't just about experiencing the world together; it was about actively shaping it, collaboratively pursuing goals that transcended personal ambitions. This collaborative spirit manifested in countless ways, big and small. We volunteered at a local homeless shelter, finding fulfillment in serving others and witnessing the transformative power of compassion firsthand. The shared satisfaction of making even a small difference in someone else's life strengthened our bond, proving that true purpose often lies not in individual achievement but in collective action. This wasn't a fleeting act of charity; it became a regular part of our lives, a testament to our shared belief in social responsibility and the importance of giving back to the community.

One significant collaborative project was the establishment of a small scholarship fund for underprivileged students. This wasn't just a financial contribution; it was a deeply personal endeavor, born from our shared conviction in the power of education to transform lives. We spent countless hours researching potential candidates, meticulously reviewing applications, and personally connecting with the students we chose to support. It was a labor of love, a tangible manifestation of our desire to leave a positive impact on the world. The joy we experienced in witnessing the success of these students, seeing their potential blossom through access to education, far surpassed any material reward. Their achievements became our achievements, a source of profound pride and shared fulfillment that underscored the depth of our partnership.

Beyond these larger-scale endeavors, our shared purpose manifested in smaller, everyday acts. We meticulously maintained our garden, nurturing plants from tiny seeds to vibrant blooms. It wasn't merely horticulture; it was a metaphor for our relationship, tending to something beautiful and fragile, requiring patience, collaboration, and a shared commitment to nurturing growth. The act of planting, weeding, and harvesting together became a ritual, a sacred space where we could connect, share our thoughts and dreams, and simply enjoy each other's company amidst the quiet beauty of nature. The fruits of our labor, literally and metaphorically, were a testament to our shared dedication and the rewards of teamwork. Even mundane tasks like household chores were transformed into opportunities for shared effort, reinforcing our sense of partnership and shared responsibility.

Our commitment to intellectual pursuits also took on a collaborative dimension. We devoured books together, engaging in lively discussions that often spilled late into the night. We attended lectures and workshops, challenging each other's perspectives and enriching our understanding of the world. These weren't solitary pursuits; they were shared journeys of discovery, strengthening our intellectual connection and stimulating our minds. Our shared love for learning fostered an environment of continuous growth, both individually and as a couple. We would meticulously curate our bookshelves, each addition a testament to a shared journey of intellectual exploration.

We also found joy in artistic endeavors, expressing our creativity together. Connie was a talented painter, and I, though less skilled, found solace in sketching and photography. We often spent afternoons in the studio, surrounded by canvases, paints, and the fragrant scent of linseed oil. These weren't simply solitary creative sessions;

they were opportunities for collaboration, offering feedback, inspiring each other, and celebrating our individual styles. The art we created, both individually and collaboratively, became a tangible representation of our shared journey, a visual tapestry woven from our collective experiences and emotions. These artworks weren't merely decorative pieces; they were precious tokens of our shared creative spirit, each stroke of paint or line a testament to our bond.

Our shared purpose wasn't confined to grand gestures or ambitious projects; it was woven into the fabric of our daily lives. It was about being each other's support system, celebrating each other's victories, and offering solace during challenging times. It was about creating a home filled with love, laughter, and shared experiences. It was about building a life that was not merely a collection of individual achievements, but a unified masterpiece created through collaboration, understanding, and unwavering commitment. Our life together wasn't simply two parallel paths converging occasionally; it was a single, intertwined journey, a testament to the profound truth that 'two bodies can truly become one soul' through shared purpose and unwavering love.

The death of Connie has left an irreplaceable void in my life, but it hasn't diminished the profound impact of our shared purpose. In fact, it has only amplified it, transforming my grief into a renewed determination to honor her legacy and continue the work we started together. The scholarship fund continues to thrive, and I remain actively involved in its administration, driven by the memory of our shared passion for education and social justice. I continue to tend our garden, finding solace in the quiet rhythm of nurturing life, a ritual that echoes our shared dedication to nurturing and growth. Even the mundane tasks that we once shared now seem imbued with a poignant significance, each one a reminder of her presence and the life we created together.

Looking back, I understand now that our shared purpose wasn't merely a goal; it was the very essence of our love. It wasn't just about achieving specific outcomes; it was about the process of striving together, supporting each other, and building something meaningful beyond ourselves. The shared laughter, the challenging discussions, the quiet moments of shared contemplation – these are the memories that sustain me now, not as fleeting moments, but as fundamental pillars of our shared identity.

The pain of loss is undeniable, a constant companion in my daily life. But interwoven with that pain is a profound sense of gratitude for the life we built together, a life filled with purpose, love, and a shared journey towards a greater good. The legacy of 'two bodies and one soul' isn't merely a romantic notion; it's a testament to the power of shared purpose, a beacon that guides me through the darkness of grief, reminding me of the enduring strength of a love that transcended individual existence. The work we started together continues, propelled by the unwavering memory of our shared dreams and aspirations, a testament to a love that death cannot erase. The vibrancy of our shared existence continues to resonate within me, not as a burden, but as a constant source of inspiration, pushing me forward, strengthening my resolve, and guiding my actions.

Connie's absence is a constant, gnawing ache, a wound that refuses to fully heal. Yet, amidst the profound sorrow, a different kind of strength emerges. It's not a stoic, emotionless resilience, but a strength born from grief, shaped by loss, and fueled by the enduring power of our shared purpose. It is a strength that acknowledges the pain, validates the sorrow, yet refuses to be consumed by it. It's a strength that finds purpose in continuing the work we began together, a strength that allows me to carry her memory not as a burden, but as a beacon illuminating my path.

Our shared life wasn't merely a collection of experiences, but a testament to the transformative power of shared intention. The projects we undertook, both large and small, weren't simply tasks to be completed; they were expressions of our values, our aspirations, and our commitment to each other and the world around us. They were tangible manifestations of our belief in the power of collaboration, the importance of giving back, and the enduring strength of a bond that transcended the physical realm. Even now, as I navigate the complexities of grief, it's these shared accomplishments, these collaborative efforts, that offer a sense of continuity, a reminder of the beautiful life we built together, a life woven from the threads of shared purpose and enduring love. The memories of our shared triumphs and challenges, the tangible results of our collaboration, serve as powerful reminders of the depth of our connection, a connection that continues to shape my life even in her absence. The work continues, driven by a profound gratitude for the life we shared, a life that stands as a testament to the unwavering power of "two bodies and one soul." It's in this continuation, in this quiet commitment to carrying forward the torch we held together, that I find solace, strength, and a renewed sense of purpose. The pain remains, a constant companion, but it's now intertwined with the enduring warmth of our shared legacy, a legacy that will continue to shape my life, a life forever touched by the profound impact of Connie's presence. And that, in itself, is a powerful testament to the enduring nature of a love built on a foundation of shared purpose. The journey continues, guided by the memory of our shared purpose, fueled by the unwavering strength of our enduring love.

## Seasons of Joy and Triumph

Our forty-one years together weren't solely defined by the quiet moments, the shared cups of tea at sunrise, or the comfortable silences that spoke volumes. They were punctuated by vibrant bursts of joy, milestones celebrated with unrestrained exuberance, and triumphs that felt as monumental as scaling the highest mountain. These weren't simply events; they were the vibrant threads woven into the rich tapestry of our life together, the vibrant colours against which the quieter shades of intimacy stood out.

Connie's graduation from law school, a moment she had strived towards with unwavering dedication, stands out as a pivotal memory. The sheer elation on her face, the pride in her eyes, were a testament to her strength and determination. It wasn't just the achievement itself; it was the journey, the late nights spent studying, the unwavering support we gave each other, that forged an unbreakable bond. We celebrated with a small gathering of close friends and family, a joyous occasion imbued with the promise of a future brimming with potential. The feeling of shared accomplishment, the quiet pride in witnessing her success, remains a cherished memory.

Then there was the purchase of our first home, a modest bungalow that we painstakingly renovated, transforming it into a haven of warmth and laughter. Each layer of paint, each carefully chosen fixture, each nail hammered into place, was an act of love and shared creation. It was more than just a house; it was a symbol of our commitment, a physical manifestation of the life we were building together, brick by brick, dream by dream. The joy of creating a home, of shaping a space that reflected our personalities and dreams, was unparalleled. It was a tangible representation of our shared journey, a foundation upon which our life continued to flourish.

Our travels were another source of profound joy. From the bustling markets of Marrakech to the serene beaches of Bali, each trip was an adventure, a shared exploration that deepened our understanding of ourselves and the world around us. We weren't just tourists; we were active participants, immersing ourselves in local cultures, engaging with people from all walks of life, and bringing back not just souvenirs, but a wealth of shared memories and experiences that enriched our lives immeasurably. The vibrant colours of a Moroccan sunset, the ancient temples of Angkor Wat, the taste of exotic fruits – each memory remains vividly alive, a testament to the joy of exploration and shared discovery.

Beyond the grand adventures, the simple joys were equally significant. The annual trips to the autumn festivals, the quiet evenings spent reading side-by-side, the spontaneous picnics in the park – these seemingly insignificant moments were the building blocks of our happiness, the daily affirmations of our enduring love. The shared laughter over a silly movie, the comfort of a shared silence, the warmth of a hug after a long day – these were the small gestures, the quiet moments of connection, that formed the bedrock of our forty-one years together.

Connie's artistic endeavors brought immense joy to our lives. Her passion for painting, her dedication to mastering her craft, was both inspiring and humbling. I vividly recall the pride I felt when her artwork was selected for a prestigious exhibition, the way she glowed with accomplishment and happiness. It wasn't just about the recognition; it was the embodiment of her artistic spirit, her unwavering commitment to her passion, that truly resonated. Watching her create, seeing her transform blank canvases into vibrant expressions of her inner world, was a privilege that enriched my life immensely. Her art, like our life together, was a vibrant expression of beauty, creativity, and unwavering spirit.

Our professional achievements were intertwined, supporting each other through challenging times and celebrating each other's successes. I was always proud of her career progression, the dedication she put into her work, and the impact she had on those around her. The success she achieved was a reflection of her hard work, determination, and exceptional intellect. There were times when work felt overwhelming, but we always managed to support each other. Even during stressful deadlines, we found time for ourselves, whether it was a quiet evening at home or a weekend escape. These moments of respite, of shared support, served as a constant reminder that we were in this together, and that our individual triumphs were also shared victories. It wasn't just about our individual achievements; it was about our collaborative spirit, our unwavering support for each other, that made our journey so fulfilling.

But these triumphs weren't solely confined to professional and personal accomplishments. They also encompassed the smaller, more intimate victories – overcoming personal challenges, navigating life's inevitable difficulties, and emerging stronger and more resilient as a couple. We faced trials and tribulations together, learning to rely on each other, to draw strength from each other's resilience, and to emerge from challenging situations with a deepened sense of understanding and compassion. These shared experiences, the collective effort to overcome obstacles, are just as valuable in shaping a lifetime of memories as are grand celebrations and monumental achievements. The strength found in the shared burden of life's harsher realities solidified the bond that held us together, weaving an even tighter tapestry of trust and love.

It wasn't always easy. There were times of doubt, moments of frustration, and periods of adjustment as our individual roles and responsibilities evolved. But we navigated these moments with grace and resilience, always emerging stronger and more deeply connected. Each challenge overcame was a victory, a testament to our unwavering commitment to each other. These struggles, these moments of shared vulnerability, served as powerful reminders of our resilience and strengthened our bond.

Our shared faith and spiritual practices provided a grounding stability throughout our lives, providing a framework for understanding the world and our place within it. We found comfort and inspiration in philosophical discussions, drawing parallels between ancient wisdom and modern experiences. The teachings of Lord Krishna, the wisdom of Chanakya – these provided not only intellectual stimulation but also a framework for navigating the complexities of life and loss. This shared spiritual framework, this common ground of faith and understanding, fostered a connection that extended beyond the physical realm, strengthening the bond that was the cornerstone of our marriage. It's a foundation that still sustains me, even in this profound grief.

Through all the seasons of joy and triumph, through the quiet moments of shared intimacy and the boisterous celebrations of shared success, one constant remained: the unwavering strength of our connection, the profound depth of our love. It was a love that transcended the mundane, that infused meaning into everyday experiences, and that shaped the very fabric of our lives. It was, quite simply, the love that defined us, and the love that continues to define me, even in her absence. The memories, the accomplishments, the shared laughter and tears – they are the threads that compose the intricate tapestry of our life together, a tapestry woven with love, dedication, and shared purpose. A testament to the reality and magic of 'two bodies and one soul.' And while the pain of her loss is a constant companion, these memories are my solace, my strength, my enduring legacy. They are the enduring flame that keeps burning bright.

The intensity of our shared life, the depth of our connection, wasn't just about grand adventures and significant accomplishments. It was about the quiet appreciation for the simple moments, the shared laughter over inside jokes, the unspoken understanding that existed between us. It was about building a life together, brick by brick, sharing not just experiences but also hopes, dreams, and anxieties. It was about being each other's safe haven, a constant source of support and encouragement. Even in the midst of life's everyday challenges, we always found a way to connect, to reaffirm our love for each other.

Looking back, I am struck by the sheer abundance of joy and fulfillment that permeated our life. It wasn't always easy; we faced our share of hardships and challenges. But even in the face of adversity, our love remained steadfast, a constant source of strength and resilience. We learned to navigate life's storms together, emerging stronger and closer than ever before. Each challenge we met, each obstacle we overcame, only served to deepen our bond and strengthen our commitment to one another. It was in those moments of shared vulnerability that our connection shone most brightly.

Our shared love wasn't just a feeling; it was a commitment, a daily practice, a conscious decision to choose each other, again and again, throughout the passage of time. It was about cherishing the small moments, celebrating the big milestones, and navigating the inevitable storms of life with grace and understanding. It was about growth, acceptance, and the constant pursuit of a shared, meaningful existence. It was about the tangible expression of love, a weaving of two lives into one cohesive, beautiful tapestry.

It's in the quiet moments of reflection, when I allow myself to delve into the depths of our shared history, that the true beauty of our life together becomes clear. It wasn't just about the grand adventures or the significant accomplishments; it was about the accumulation of countless small moments, the quiet gestures of love and support, the unspoken understanding that existed between us. It was a symphony of shared experiences, a harmonious blend of two souls intertwined, creating a melody of life that continues to resonate within me.

The pain of her loss is still profoundly acute, a constant reminder of the void left in my life. Yet, amidst the sorrow, I find solace in the abundance of joy and fulfillment that defined our life together. Those memories, the vibrant tapestry of shared experiences, provide a constant source of strength and comfort. They are the remnants of a love so deep, so profound, that even death cannot fully extinguish its flame. It burns on, a testament to the enduring power of love, a beacon guiding me through the darkest of nights. And in remembering, in cherishing, in sharing, I find a way to carry her light forward. It's a legacy of love, a testament to a life well-lived, a life woven from the threads of two bodies and one soul.

# The Unseen Threads of Destiny

The notion that Connie and I were destined to be together, that our union was something more profound than mere chance, has been a constant companion throughout my grief. It wasn't a belief imposed upon us by religious dogma or societal pressure; it was an intuitive understanding that blossomed over decades, a quiet certainty that resonated deep within our souls. We didn't meet in a whirlwind romance, a dramatic collision of fate. Our connection unfolded more gradually, like the slow, steady growth of an ancient oak, its roots intertwining deeply beneath the surface.

We met at a university lecture on ancient Indian philosophy. I remember vividly the way the afternoon sun streamed through the tall windows, illuminating the dust motes dancing in the air. Connie, sitting a few rows ahead, captivated me not with any striking beauty but with the intensity of her focus, the way her brow furrowed in concentration as the lecturer spoke of karma and dharma. There was a quiet intellectual curiosity about her that mirrored my own, a thirst for knowledge and understanding that transcended the superficial. It wasn't love at first sight, not in the cinematic sense; it was a recognition, a silent acknowledgment of kindred spirits.

Over the next few months, our conversations became increasingly deeper, extending far beyond the confines of academia. We debated the intricacies of existentialism, the complexities of human nature, the enduring power of love and loss. Our discussions often stretched late into the night, fueled by strong coffee and a shared fascination with the mysteries of the universe. We found a comfort in each other's presence, a sense of belonging that transcended the usual social niceties. It was as if we had known each other in a previous life, a past existence where our souls had danced in harmony.

This sense of destiny deepened with each passing year. Our lives unfolded in a manner that felt both planned and serendipitous. Opportunities appeared as if guided by an unseen hand, challenges arose and were overcome as if by a pre-ordained plan. We navigated life's complexities together, our paths diverging and converging in ways that felt almost magical. The synchronicity was uncanny, a constant reminder of the unique bond that held us together. A shared love for travel led us to remote corners of the world, from the serene temples of Kyoto to the bustling souks of Marrakech. Each journey seemed to enhance our connection, deepening our understanding of both ourselves and each other. Our shared passion for art filled our home with vibrant colours and evocative forms, reflecting the rich tapestry of our lives together.

Even the challenges we faced—the financial struggles of our early years, the stress of raising a family, the anxieties of navigating professional careers—seemed to strengthen our bond. We faced each adversity hand-in-hand, drawing strength from our shared faith in a larger, more benevolent plan. We often discussed the philosophy of Chanakya, the ancient Indian strategist whose teachings emphasized the importance of resilience, resourcefulness and clear vision. His emphasis on pragmatism and foresight resonated deeply with us. We applied his principles not only to our careers but also to our relationship, navigating the complexities of life with a shared sense of purpose and determination.

Our spiritual journey also played a significant role in solidifying our belief in destiny. We delved deeply into various spiritual traditions, drawing inspiration from the Bhagavad Gita, the teachings of Lord Krishna and the profound wisdom of the Upanishads. The concept of "yoga," the union of body, mind, and spirit, became a central theme in our lives, a guiding principle for navigating the complexities of our emotional and spiritual landscape. The Gita's message of selfless action and surrendering to the divine will offered solace during challenging times, reinforcing our belief in a larger cosmic plan.

The unwavering support we offered each other throughout our lives reinforced this sense of predestination. In times of uncertainty or crisis—be it professional setbacks, health scares, or personal challenges—we turned to each other for comfort and guidance. My background in crisis management provided a framework for navigating difficult situations, but Connie's unwavering faith and spiritual strength always provided the emotional anchor we needed. Our crisis management was less a matter of checklists and procedures and more about supporting each other through love and empathy. We were each other's refuge, our anchor in the storms of life.

And yet, the unshakeable belief in our destiny didn't shield us from the inevitable heartbreak of loss. Connie's illness and subsequent death shattered my world. The pain was, and remains, unbearable. The anger at the alleged medical negligence that contributed to her suffering fueled a fire within me—a burning desire for justice, for accountability. It was as if the very threads of destiny had been cruelly severed, a tapestry ripped asunder.

However, even in the depths of my despair, the conviction of our destined union remains. It doesn't diminish the pain, nor does it erase the anger. Instead, it offers a different perspective, a framework through which I can process my grief. It suggests that our time together, though tragically shortened, was profoundly meaningful, a testament to a love that transcended the physical realm. It was a love sculpted not merely by earthly events, but guided by forces beyond our comprehension.

Reflecting on our forty-one years, I see the unmistakable fingerprints of destiny—the seemingly coincidental meetings, the unexpected opportunities, the unwavering support we offered each other. Each moment, each challenge, each triumph, contributed to the intricate tapestry of our lives, a testament to a love that was both extraordinary and, in its own way, inevitable. The threads may have been severed, but the pattern, the beautiful, intricate design woven by our lives together, remains etched in my memory and in my heart. The vibrant colours of our shared journey, though dimmed by sorrow, continue to illuminate my path, a beacon guiding me through the darkness, reminding me that our union was not a mere accident of birth or chance encounter, but a sacred dance of souls, a destined meeting of two bodies and one soul. This understanding is not a simple explanation of our relationship; it's a living, breathing truth that sustains me in the face of overwhelming loss, a comforting thought when the silence is deafening. It is the legacy of a life shared, a destiny fulfilled, even amidst the profound sorrow.

The justice I seek is not merely about holding those responsible for Connie's suffering accountable. It's about ensuring that others do not suffer in the same way. It's about honoring her memory, not just by grieving her loss, but by using my experience to advocate for better medical practices, for greater transparency, and for increased patient safety. This is also part of our shared destiny – my role in seeking justice is a continuation of our commitment to fairness and equity. Connie always had a deep-seated sense of justice; her compassion extended far beyond our immediate world. She believed in speaking truth to power, in advocating for those who were unable to advocate for themselves. That same spirit drives me now, fuels my quest for justice, and transforms my grief into a powerful force for positive change. It is a legacy we built together; a responsibility I bear with both sorrow and determination.

Our shared love of philosophy, particularly the concepts of dharma and karma, continues to resonate deeply. The concept of dharma, one's duty or purpose in life, takes on a new meaning in the wake of loss. My dharma now, it seems, is to honor Connie's memory, to seek justice, to share our story, and to ensure that our legacy continues to inspire and empower others. The concept of karma, the notion that actions have consequences, extends beyond individual lives. It suggests a broader interconnectedness, a cosmic tapestry of cause and effect that extends far beyond our comprehension. The injustice Connie faced, the pain we endured, is part of this larger tapestry. And my pursuit of justice, my efforts to make a difference, are my response to that karma, my attempt to weave a more positive thread into the intricate pattern of life.

The pain of Connie's loss continues to be a constant presence in my life, a deep wound that may never fully heal. But the vibrant memories of our life together, the shared experiences, the intellectual discussions, the unwavering support we offered each other – these are the threads that weave a tapestry of love, resilience, and faith. These memories are not simply relics of the past; they are the living essence of our bond, a reminder that our love was not a fleeting moment but a profound and lasting connection. And in the midst of my grief, I find solace in the understanding that our union was a testament to the unseen threads of destiny, a cosmic dance of souls destined to meet, to love, to grow together, and to leave behind a legacy that echoes far beyond the limitations of time and space. The love we shared, the life we lived, transcends even death. And in that, I find an enduring peace, a quiet acceptance of the beautiful and tragic tapestry that is life.

## The Diagnosis and its Impact

The world tilted on its axis the day the oncologist uttered the words, "It's cancer." The air in the sterile office seemed to thicken, each syllable a lead weight settling in my gut. Connie, my Connie, vibrant, witty, the woman who had been my anchor for forty-one years, was facing a battle against a relentless enemy. The news wasn't a surprise, not entirely. The persistent cough, the fatigue that wouldn't lift, the subtle changes in her demeanour – these had been whispers of the storm brewing within. But whispers are different from the roar of confirmation. That roar shattered the tranquility of our life, sending shockwaves through every carefully constructed aspect of our shared existence.

The initial impact was a numbing paralysis. Forty-one years. A lifetime woven together, thread by thread, into a tapestry of shared dreams, unspoken understandings, and a love so profound it defied definition. That lifetime, that tapestry, felt suddenly fragile, threatened by an invisible force that was already beginning to unravel it. The practicalities of life, which had always been managed with a quiet efficiency between us, were now daunting obstacles. Medical appointments, consultations, the stark reality of treatment plans – these replaced the gentle rhythm of our days, the spontaneous laughter over a shared cup of tea, the quiet evenings spent reading side-by-side.

The emotional upheaval was even more profound. Fear, a chilling companion, crept into the corners of our hearts. The fear wasn't just of the disease itself, but of the unknown, of the potential loss of the woman who was inextricably intertwined with my very being. It was a fear of the future, a future now shrouded in uncertainty, where every day brought a fresh wave of anxieties, each more terrifying than the last. It was the fear of facing a life without her, the crippling thought of a world stripped of her presence, her voice, her laughter, her touch.

Connie, ever the pragmatist, faced the diagnosis with her characteristic grace and courage. Yet, I could see the fear lurking beneath the surface, a vulnerability that tugged at my heart. We were a team, always had been. We'd faced life's challenges together, weathering storms both large and small. This, however, was a storm unlike any we'd encountered before. It was a battle against an unseen adversary, a battle fought not on the battlefield but within the delicate confines of her own body.

Our shared journey through the labyrinth of medical treatment became a testament to our enduring love. Each hospital visit, each examination, each infusion, served as a stark reminder of the enemy we were fighting. The sterile environment, the hushed tones of the medical staff, the constant monitoring of vital signs, these created an atmosphere that felt simultaneously clinical and deeply personal. We clung to each other, our hands clasped tightly, seeking solace in the warmth of our shared presence. But there were moments, fleeting yet searing, when the fear would overwhelm, when the weight of the situation would crush us both under its relentless pressure.

The treatment was arduous. Chemotherapy sapped Connie's energy, leaving her weak and vulnerable. The side effects were brutal – nausea, hair loss, debilitating fatigue. She battled through it all with an unwavering spirit, but there were days when even her resilience faltered, days when the pain was simply too much to bear. I, armed with my experience in crisis management, tried to provide both emotional and practical support, meticulously organizing her care, managing her medication, anticipating her needs before she even voiced them. Yet, there were times when I felt helpless, a spectator in the unfolding tragedy, powerless to alleviate her suffering.

The uncertainty gnawed at us both. The medical prognoses offered a range of possibilities, each one more daunting than the last. We clung to hope, clinging to the positive scenarios, even as the shadows of the negative ones loomed large. Yet, it was a fragile hope, constantly tested by the harsh reality of Connie's deteriorating condition. The initial optimism began to erode, replaced by a grim awareness of the potential outcome. It was a delicate dance between hope and despair, a constant negotiation with the unpredictable nature of the illness.

During this period, we found solace in our faith and our shared philosophical perspectives. For Connie, it was a quiet, unwavering faith in a benevolent higher power. For me, it was the wisdom gleaned from years of studying spiritual and philosophical teachings. Lord Krishna's teachings on acceptance and surrender provided a framework for navigating the emotional turmoil. Chanakya's emphasis on duty and perseverance, even in the face of adversity, strengthened our resolve. We discussed these principles often, finding comfort in their timeless wisdom, their ability to offer perspective amidst the chaos.

We drew strength from each other, our love a beacon illuminating the darkest corners of our despair. We shared memories, reliving the joy and laughter of our past, cherishing the moments that had shaped our lives together. We spoke of the future, painting idealized pictures of a life beyond the illness, even as the present held a grim reality. These conversations, these moments of shared intimacy, served as anchors in the turbulent sea of uncertainty, reaffirming the strength of our bond, a bond that transcended the illness and the looming threat of loss. It was during these intimate times that the depth of our love, often subtly expressed in everyday gestures and unspoken understanding, became a palpable force, a testament to our forty-one years together, a fortress against the encroaching darkness. We held onto each other, not just as husband and wife, but as two souls inextricably intertwined, navigating life's most challenging storm together. And yet, even as we stood together, the shadow of impending loss stretched its long, cold fingers, reaching towards us both.

The diagnosis, in its stark simplicity, had not only challenged our physical and emotional well-being but also exposed the vulnerability inherent in the human condition. It stripped away the illusion of control, reminding us of life's inherent fragility. It forced us to confront our mortality, to acknowledge the inevitable end that awaited us all. It was in this stark confrontation with the finite nature of life that we truly began to appreciate the profound value of each shared moment, the preciousness of the time we had left. We began to consciously and deliberately savor the small joys, the quiet moments of connection, the simple gestures of love and affection. The illness, in its cruel way, became a catalyst for a deeper appreciation of the ephemeral nature of life, intensifying the profound love we shared. This realization, in itself, became a source of unexpected strength, even in the face of the encroaching darkness. It was a poignant reminder of the beauty and fragility of human existence, and the enduring power of love in the face of certain mortality.

## Navigating Treatment and Uncertainty

The initial shock gave way to a relentless barrage of appointments, tests, and procedures. The sterile scent of antiseptic became a constant companion, clinging to our clothes, our skin, our very memories. Connie's once vibrant laughter was replaced by the weary sighs of exhaustion, the pained whimpers during treatments. Each chemotherapy session was a brutal assault, leaving her weakened, nauseous, and emotionally drained. The vibrant woman who had once effortlessly navigated life with grace and elegance was now frail, dependent on others for even the simplest tasks. Watching her struggle, witnessing the gradual erosion of her strength, was a torture that no amount of philosophical reflection could fully alleviate. My own emotional state mirrored the roller coaster of her physical condition – moments of desperate hope punctuated by crushing waves of despair.

The hospital became our second home. The sterile white walls, the incessant beeping of machines, the hushed whispers of nurses – these formed the bleak backdrop to our shared ordeal. While Connie battled the disease, I navigated the labyrinthine corridors of the medical system, a system that felt both compassionate and callous, efficient and maddeningly bureaucratic. I learned the language of medical jargon, the intricacies of insurance claims, the art of negotiating with doctors and nurses. I became an expert in deciphering test results, a silent warrior fighting for my wife's well-being amidst the sterile, clinical environment.

Beyond the physical challenges, the emotional toll was immense. The fear, the uncertainty, the sheer helplessness— these gnawed at my soul. Sleep became a luxury, replaced by restless nights spent watching over Connie, my hand resting on hers, offering a silent vigil against the encroaching darkness. The burden of responsibility weighed heavily upon me – not just the practical aspects of her care, but also the emotional burden of bearing witness to her suffering. I found myself wrestling with conflicting emotions—the rage at the disease, the grief at the inevitable outcome, and the overwhelming love that bound us together. It was a relentless internal war, fought in the quiet moments between treatments, in the hushed hours of the night.

The uncertainty surrounding Connie's treatment was perhaps the most agonizing aspect of the entire ordeal. The doctors, despite their expertise, couldn't offer guarantees. Each test result brought with it a fresh wave of anxiety, each prognosis a gamble with fate. The initial optimism, so carefully cultivated, gradually eroded, replaced by a gnawing fear that crept into every corner of our lives. We clung to hope, but it was a fragile hope, easily shattered by the slightest setback. The uncertainty cast a long shadow over our days, making even the simplest decisions fraught with anxieties. Would this treatment work? Would there be more to come? Would we have more time together? These questions hung heavy in the air, unspoken yet omnipresent.

Our conversations shifted subtly, reflecting the gravity of our situation. We spoke less about plans for the future, more about memories of the past. We revisited cherished moments, replaying our favorite memories like precious film reels, each scene a testament to the depth of our love. These conversations, although tinged with sadness, provided a strange form of solace, a quiet acknowledgment of the preciousness of our shared time. They were a way of holding on, of preserving the essence of our relationship amidst the looming shadow of death. We found comfort in these shared reflections, a profound understanding and acceptance of our mortality, a testament to the resilience of our bond.

The initial optimism we'd clung to after the initial diagnosis gradually gave way to a more realistic assessment of our situation. The medical professionals, while compassionate, were also realistic about the severity of Connie's condition. They were careful not to offer false hope, but neither did they shy away from the difficult conversations about end-of-life care. These conversations were harrowing, each one stripping away another layer of denial, revealing the stark reality of our situation. They were uncomfortable, deeply unsettling, but necessary. They forced me to confront the inevitability of Connie's passing, to prepare myself for a future that would be forever altered by her absence. This preparation, though painful, became a strange form of strength; it allowed me to focus on cherishing every moment we had left.

The medical professionals, while skilled and dedicated, couldn't always provide the answers we sought. The complexity of Connie's illness, the unpredictable nature of cancer, made it impossible to predict the course of her treatment. There were moments of progress, followed by setbacks. We learned to ride the waves of uncertainty, clinging to hope amidst the storms of despair. It was during this time that I began to question the system itself. I started to notice inconsistencies in the information we received, delays in treatment, missed opportunities that could have potentially improved her condition. This fueled a growing sense of unease, a sense of injustice that would later propel me to seek accountability.

Yet, amidst the uncertainty, love remained our constant. In the quiet moments between treatments, we shared a depth of intimacy that transcended words. The illness, paradoxically, had strengthened our bond, reminding us of the fragility of life and the preciousness of love. Simple gestures, a shared glance, a tender touch – these became acts of profound significance, reaffirming our commitment to each other. We found solace in our shared faith, drawing strength from our spiritual beliefs and philosophical understandings. We reflected on the impermanence of life, on the eternal nature of the soul, and the interconnectedness of all things. These reflections provided a sense of perspective, a grounding in the midst of chaos.

Throughout this ordeal, my faith in humanity was constantly challenged and yet, at the same time, surprisingly reinforced. While the bureaucratic hurdles of the healthcare system often felt like insurmountable obstacles, the compassion and dedication of certain individuals stood out in stark contrast. The nurses who went above and beyond their duties, who offered words of comfort and support, who treated Connie with dignity and respect – these were beacons of hope in a world often defined by its clinical detachment. These experiences underscored the importance of human connection, the power of empathy, and the enduring strength of the human spirit in the face of adversity. These were the moments that kept my hope alive, that gave me strength to continue fighting, not just for Connie's well-being, but also for a more humane and compassionate healthcare system.

The financial burden of Connie's illness was also significant. The cost of treatment, medication, hospital stays, and travel added up quickly, straining our resources. We had carefully planned for our retirement, but the unexpected illness threw those plans into disarray. It wasn't just the financial strain; it was the added stress of worrying about bills, insurance coverage, and the potential depletion of our savings. This financial pressure exacerbated the emotional burden, adding another layer of anxiety to an already difficult situation. The disparity between the life-saving treatment and its exorbitant cost was a stark reminder of the inequalities within the healthcare system. It raised questions about access to quality healthcare and the ethical implications of prioritizing profit over patient well-being.

The experience of navigating Connie's illness taught me invaluable lessons. I learned the importance of advocacy, the need to be a vigilant guardian of one's own health and the health of loved ones. I learned the limitations of the medical system, the frustrating inefficiencies, and the heartbreaking unpredictability of illness. But most importantly, I learned the enduring power of love, the unwavering strength of the human spirit, and the preciousness of every shared moment. The journey was excruciating, filled with pain and loss, but it was also a testament to the resilience of the human heart, the depth of human connection, and the enduring power of love in the face of death. It was a journey that would irrevocably change me, shaping my perspectives on life, death, and the world around me. And it is a journey I share here, not just as a personal testament to Connie's life and our love, but also as a plea for a more compassionate and just healthcare system, a system that prioritizes human dignity and well-being above all else.

## Maintaining Hope Amidst Despair

The sterile white walls of the hospital room seemed to press in on me, a stark contrast to the vibrant tapestry of our life together. Connie, my Connie, lay frail, the vibrant spark in her eyes dimmed, replaced by a weary acceptance. Yet, even in the face of such overwhelming despair, I refused to surrender to hopelessness. Hope, I realized, wasn't the absence of fear or pain, but a stubborn refusal to let those emotions define us. It was a conscious choice, a daily practice, a flickering flame that I had to nurture against the relentless winds of grief.

One of the tools I employed, ironically given the circumstances, was my background in crisis management. I approached Connie's illness with a methodical, almost clinical precision, compartmentalizing my emotions to create space for rational decision-making. This wasn't about detaching from my feelings, but about channeling my energy into effective action. I meticulously researched treatment options, consulted with leading oncologists, and became a fierce advocate for Connie's well-being within the often-opaque medical system. This proactive approach, while demanding and emotionally taxing, gave me a sense of control in a situation where I felt utterly powerless. It provided a tangible outlet for my anxieties, transforming my helplessness into purposeful activity.

The support of family and friends became our lifeline, a tangible manifestation of the love and compassion that surrounded us. My children, ever resilient, rallied around their mother, offering comfort, support, and a much-needed sense of normalcy amidst the chaos. Friends brought meals, offered childcare, and simply sat with us, providing companionship and a silent acknowledgment of our shared pain. These acts of kindness, often small and unassuming, were profound expressions of love and solidarity, bolstering our spirits and reminding us that we were not alone in this fight. Their presence was a constant reassurance that even in the darkest hours, we were enveloped in a network of love and support.

I drew strength from unexpected sources too. My long-standing interest in philosophy and spirituality provided a framework for understanding our situation. The Bhagavad Gita, with its teachings on dharma (duty) and karma (action), became a source of comfort and guidance. Krishna's message of selfless action resonated deeply, reminding me that even amidst suffering, we had a responsibility to live with grace and dignity. The teachings of Chanakya, the ancient Indian strategist and philosopher, helped me navigate the complex ethical dilemmas that arose from the alleged medical negligence we faced. His emphasis on justice and accountability fueled my determination to seek redress for Connie's suffering, transforming my grief into a powerful impetus for action.

Beyond philosophical insights, I found solace in the simple beauty of everyday life. The gentle caress of sunlight on my skin, the symphony of birdsong in the morning, the warmth of a shared cup of tea – these small moments became precious reminders of the enduring beauty of the world, even amidst pain and loss. We cultivated small rituals, creating pockets of normalcy and joy within the overwhelming reality of Connie's illness. We watched sunsets together, listened to our favorite music, read poetry aloud, and shared stories of our life together, savoring each precious moment as if it were our last. These shared experiences strengthened our bond, creating a tapestry of shared memories that continue to sustain me even now.

The support extended beyond our immediate circle. Unexpected acts of kindness from strangers, a handwritten note of encouragement, a sympathetic glance from a fellow patient's family member, all contributed to a feeling of collective empathy and shared humanity. These seemingly insignificant gestures served as powerful reminders that our struggle was not isolated, that we were part of a larger human experience. It reinforced my belief in the inherent goodness of people, a belief that became increasingly important during a time of profound adversity.

Despite our efforts to maintain a positive outlook, moments of despair were inevitable. The crushing weight of grief would sometimes overwhelm me, threatening to extinguish the flickering flame of hope. During these times, I learned the importance of self-compassion and allowing myself to feel the full spectrum of emotions without judgment. I recognized that suppressing my grief would only prolong the healing process. Instead, I embraced the tears, the anger, the frustration, allowing myself to experience the full force of my emotions without attempting to control or deny them.

But even in the depths of despair, a persistent thread of hope remained. It wasn't a naïve optimism, but a grounded faith in the enduring power of love and the resilience of the human spirit. This hope wasn't about expecting a miraculous cure or a sudden reversal of fate, but about accepting the reality of our situation while simultaneously cherishing the precious moments we had left. It was a hope rooted in the profound connection I shared with Connie, a bond that transcended the boundaries of life and death. It was a hope that sustained me through the darkest hours, guiding me through the labyrinth of grief towards a future where, though changed, I could find a path forward, honoring the memory of our love and the lessons we learned together. This hope, nurtured through faith, philosophy, love and support, became my anchor, my guide, my constant companion through the turbulent waters of grief. It continues to be the guiding force in my life, a testament to the enduring power of the human spirit in the face of profound loss. The pain of loss remains, but it is tempered by the enduring legacy of our love, a love that continues to shape my life and guide my actions even now. And that, in itself, is a form of hope – a hope born not of denial, but of acceptance and unwavering love.

# The Crushing Weight of Fear

The initial shock of Connie's diagnosis had given way to a creeping, insidious fear. It wasn't a sudden, overwhelming terror, but a slow, relentless erosion of my peace of mind, a gnawing anxiety that burrowed its way into every waking moment. It was the fear of the unknown, the uncertainty of what the future held. Would she survive? How long did we have? Would her suffering be prolonged and unbearable? These questions, unanswered and unanswerable, hung heavy in the air, a suffocating blanket of dread.

My background in crisis management, usually a source of strength and control, felt utterly useless against the onslaught of this fear. I had managed countless crises, navigated complex situations, and brought order to chaos. But this was different. This was personal, visceral, a direct assault on everything I held dear. My rational mind struggled to cope with the irrationality of it all. The meticulously crafted plans and contingency strategies I relied on in my professional life offered no solace here. They were as fragile and inadequate as a paper boat in a hurricane.

The fear wasn't just about Connie's physical suffering; it was about the loss of her, the potential annihilation of our shared world. Forty-one years. Forty-one years of laughter, shared dreams, whispered secrets, and the unwavering comfort of her presence. Forty-one years woven into the very fabric of my being. The thought of a life without her was unbearable, a void so vast it threatened to swallow me whole. It was the fear of solitude, of an echoing silence that would forever replace her vibrant voice, her infectious laugh, her insightful observations. It was the chilling prospect of a future where her warmth and love, the very essence of my life, would be absent.

The anxiety manifested in unexpected ways. Sleep became a battlefield, haunted by vivid, disturbing dreams. I would jolt awake in a cold sweat, my heart pounding, the images of Connie's weakened form seared into my memory. The days were a blur of appointments, consultations, treatments, each one a fresh wave of apprehension. Even the simple act of making a cup of tea, a routine ritual we had shared for decades, became a painful reminder of her absence, a stark symbol of the life we were losing.

The weight of responsibility pressed down on me, adding another layer to the existing fear. Connie, always practical and organized, had meticulously documented her wishes, but the sheer volume of decisions that needed to be made – medical, financial, legal – felt overwhelming. I found myself struggling to make even the simplest choices, paralyzed by fear of making the wrong one, of failing her in some way. Each decision felt fraught with significance, amplified by the knowledge that every choice I made would shape the remaining moments of her life, and would profoundly impact my own future.

The uncertainty about the future added another dimension to my fear. Would I be able to cope with life alone? Would I ever find a sense of normalcy again? Would the pain ever lessen? Would the memories become less sharp, less agonizing? These questions were tormenting, their answers hidden behind a veil of uncertainty. The future, once a tapestry woven with dreams and aspirations, now seemed like a vast, dark expanse, an uncharted territory filled with unknown dangers.

My faith, usually a source of comfort and strength, felt strangely inadequate. While I found solace in spiritual practices, the raw, visceral fear refused to be subdued by philosophical musings. I spent countless hours reading scriptures, seeking answers, meditating, trying to find peace in the midst of the storm. Yet, the fear persisted, a constant companion that shadowed every aspect of my life.

The medical professionals, while competent and caring, could not alleviate this deep-seated fear. Their reassurances, though well-intentioned, felt hollow, incapable of addressing the profound emotional turmoil I was experiencing. I understood their limitations, yet I longed for something more, a magic wand that could erase the fear, a promise of a future free from pain. The rational part of my brain understood the medical complexities, the probabilities, the limitations of medicine. But the emotional part raged, grasping for answers, for certainty, for hope in the face of an uncertain destiny.

My anger, a simmering volcano beneath the surface of my fear, occasionally erupted. The anger was directed not just at the disease that ravaged Connie's body, but also at the perceived negligence, the missed opportunities, the possible mistakes that may have contributed to her suffering. This was not simply grief; it was a profound injustice, a violation of trust, a violation of our shared life. The anger fueled my determination to seek justice, to ensure that no other family had to endure the same pain and uncertainty.

Even in my moments of intense fear, the memory of our forty-one years together became a lifeline, a source of unexpected strength. I would recall our travels, our shared passions, the quiet moments of intimacy and understanding. These memories, precious jewels amidst the rubble of my present reality, reminded me of the depth and richness of our life together. They fueled my determination to fight for Connie, to honor her memory, and to find a way to navigate the treacherous waters of grief. The fear never fully dissipated, but it was gradually tempered by the enduring power of our love, a testament to the bond we shared, a bond that transcended the boundaries of life and death.

The fear remained a constant companion, a shadow that clung to me, but it no longer held the same power. I learned to live with it, to acknowledge its presence without allowing it to dictate my actions or define my life. I discovered that facing my fears, confronting them head-on, was the only way to begin to heal. It wasn't about erasing the fear, but about integrating it into my experience, understanding it as a natural response to the profound loss I was facing. It was a process, a journey, a slow but steady progression towards acceptance, a gradual shift from the crushing weight of fear to a more manageable, if still painful, awareness of my loss and my new reality. My hope, my faith, and the enduring legacy of our love became the anchors that held me steady in the storm, guiding me through the darkness towards a future where Connie's memory would forever be a source of both profound sadness and enduring love. The journey was arduous, but the love we shared, the lessons we learned together, and the unwavering commitment to seeking justice became the guiding lights that illuminated my path through the darkness. The fear remained, a constant reminder of my loss, but it was now merely a part of my story, not the entire narrative.

# Spiritual Coping Mechanisms

The relentless assault of Connie's illness forced me to confront not only the fragility of life but also the profound limitations of purely material comforts. The best medical care, the most comfortable surroundings, even the unwavering support of family and friends – none of these could truly mitigate the suffering that consumed her, and by extension, consumed me. It was during this agonizing period that I found myself increasingly drawn to spiritual and philosophical frameworks that offered solace far beyond the reach of modern medicine.

My upbringing, steeped in the traditions of India, provided a natural foundation for this exploration. The Bhagavad Gita, a sacred text that had been a silent companion throughout my life, took on new urgency and profound meaning. Krishna's counsel on dharma, the righteous path of duty, resonated deeply. My duty, I realized, wasn't just to be by Connie's side, physically tending to her needs, but also to remain steadfast in my love and support, to navigate the emotional and spiritual turbulence with as much grace and strength as I could muster. It wasn't about escaping the reality of her suffering, but about finding meaning and purpose within it. This wasn't about religious piety; it was about finding a framework for understanding, for coping, for maintaining some semblance of inner peace amidst the chaos.

The concept of karma, the law of cause and effect, also became a significant lens through which I viewed Connie's illness. While I wrestled with anger and resentment towards those I believed had contributed to her suffering – the alleged medical negligence, the system that seemed designed to prioritize profit over patient well-being – the idea of karma provided a framework for understanding, not necessarily excusing, the events unfolding around us. It wasn't about assigning blame or seeking retribution, but about accepting the present moment, learning from the experiences, and striving to create positive change for the future. This was not a passive acceptance of fate; it was an active engagement with the present, fueled by the desire for justice and fueled by the memory of Connie's indomitable spirit.

Beyond the Gita, I found solace in the philosophies of Chanakya, the ancient Indian strategist and statesman. His emphasis on pragmatism and rational decision-making proved surprisingly helpful in navigating the complex and emotionally charged landscape of Connie's illness. Chanakya's wisdom helped me to approach each challenge with a clear head, to make practical decisions, even when my emotions threatened to overwhelm me. It was a matter of separating the emotional turmoil from the practical needs of the situation, of creating a balance between the heart's yearning and the mind's practical considerations. This wasn't about suppressing emotions; it was about acknowledging their presence while maintaining the capacity for decisive and effective action. This was about strategic thinking to ensure her well-being amidst the uncertainty.

The Stoic philosophy, with its emphasis on accepting what we cannot control and focusing on what we can, also provided a powerful framework for coping with the overwhelming nature of Connie's illness. There was a profound irony in this: the illness was something I could not control, yet Stoic principles provided me the mental fortitude to manage the situation. The acceptance of what I could not control—Connie's illness and its inevitable progression—allowed me to focus my energy on what I could control: my emotional response, my actions, my commitment to her care, and the relentless pursuit of justice for the negligence that I believed hastened her end. This wasn't passive resignation; it was an active engagement with the present moment, drawing strength from the control I had over my own responses. This was the power of self-mastery.

During this challenging time, meditation became an essential anchor for my emotional well-being. It wasn't about achieving some transcendental state, but about finding a space of stillness and clarity amidst the storm. In those quiet moments, I could connect with Connie's presence, not just as a memory, but as a sustaining force within my being. These moments of meditation provided pockets of peace in the midst of chaos, a safe harbor from the emotional waves that threatened to overwhelm me.

The quiet moments were not always about Connie. There were times when I needed to focus on my own breathing, my own existence, my own capacity to endure. This was not about escaping from the grief but about creating a sanctuary where I could access the strength to navigate the day, to provide the best care for Connie, and to manage the mounting challenges of her illness. The practice of mindfulness, of being fully present in each moment, however painful, helped me to avoid getting lost in the maelstrom of fear and anxiety that threatened to consume me. It was a constant practice, a daily discipline, a way of honoring both Connie and myself.

The spiritual practices, however, were not a panacea; they did not erase my grief or eliminate the pain. The pain remained raw, visceral, ever-present. But they did provide a context, a framework for understanding, a source of strength to navigate the turbulent waters of loss. They helped me find meaning and purpose amidst the suffering, a path through the darkness that led to a future where Connie's memory, while forever tinged with sadness, would remain a beacon of enduring love, a powerful catalyst for seeking justice, and a testament to the profound bond we shared—a bond that transcended the physical realm and resided in the depths of our souls.

Our shared love of art and music became an unexpected source of solace. We'd always found comfort in the beauty of a painting, the soaring notes of an opera, or the quiet intimacy of a favorite song. Even in Connie's weakened state, we'd listen to music together, finding solace in the shared experience of beauty, a shared appreciation for the transcendent power of art to transcend the boundaries of physical suffering. These shared experiences became touchstones, reminding me of the enduring connection we shared, a bond that even death could not sever.

These spiritual and philosophical practices did not magically resolve my grief or provide easy answers. The pain was always there; it never disappeared. It was a constant companion, a shadow that followed me. But these practices gave me a framework to understand it, to contextualize it, to manage it without allowing it to completely consume me. It was about finding a way to live with the pain, to integrate it into my being, while maintaining a capacity for joy, for love, for hope, and for the ongoing pursuit of justice for Connie. It was a process of evolving, of adapting, of learning to live with the loss while cherishing the memory of an extraordinary love. This was the journey, the continuing work, the testament to the power of love, the quest for meaning, and the unending search for a future where Connie's spirit and her love continue to inform my life. And it was a journey that was profoundly spiritual, profoundly personal, and profoundly transformative.

# The Final Moments

The sterile scent of antiseptic still clings to my memory, a phantom smell that accompanies the echoing silence of the room. It was a Tuesday, the afternoon sun casting long shadows across the pale hospital walls, a stark contrast to the darkness that was descending upon my world. Connie's breathing, once the steady rhythm of our shared life, had become shallow, ragged, a heartbreaking whisper against the beeping of the machines that were now her only companions. Her hand, usually warm and comforting, was cold, the skin paper-thin, translucent. I held it, my own trembling, a desperate attempt to anchor myself to something tangible, something real, in the face of the terrifying unreal. Her eyes, usually sparkling with intelligence and humor, were closed, a final curtain drawn on a life that had been so vibrant, so full of love.

The doctor's words, delivered with a practiced but nonetheless jarring detachment, sliced through the fog of my grief. "She's gone," he said, his voice a low monotone that seemed to echo the emptiness that was already spreading through my soul. Gone. The word itself felt inadequate, a pale reflection of the gaping void that had suddenly opened up in my life, swallowing everything in its path. Forty-one years. Forty-one years of shared laughter, whispered secrets, passionate arguments, and unwavering devotion. Forty-one years that had been reduced to a single, devastating sentence.

I didn't cry at that moment. The shock was so profound, so complete, that it paralyzed me. It was as if a switch had been flipped, plunging me into a state of numb disbelief. The world continued around me, but I was detached from it, an observer watching a movie that held no meaning, no relevance. The nurses fussed around, making preparations, their actions muted, almost ghostly, against the backdrop of my emotional paralysis. I felt a strange sense of detachment, a kind of professional observation born from years spent managing crises – a perspective that felt both helpful and utterly inappropriate in this deeply personal tragedy. My mind, trained to assess, analyze, and strategize, struggled to process the raw, unfiltered pain.

Later, as they wheeled Connie's lifeless body away, the reality began to seep in, slowly, agonizingly. The tears finally came, not in a torrent, but in a steady stream that seemed to drain the very essence of my being. They were tears of profound loss, tears of unfathomable grief, tears of rage against a cruel and indifferent universe. I slumped onto a chair in the waiting area, the fluorescent lights buzzing overhead like angry wasps, each hum a tiny jab of pain. The world outside, with its bustling traffic and oblivious chatter, felt like a cruel mockery, a symphony of noise playing against the silence in my heart.

The days that followed blurred into a chaotic haze of funeral arrangements, condolences, and a relentless tide of paperwork. The legal aspects, the practicalities of death, intruded upon my grief, demanding attention even as my soul screamed for respite. I found myself navigating a maze of bureaucracy, the very system designed to offer support, ironically adding to my burden. Each form, each signature, was a painful reminder of Connie's absence, a fresh wound opened and rubbed with salt. My mind, accustomed to managing complexities, now wrestled with the insurmountable complexity of grief, a problem with no easy solution, no clear path to resolution.

The emptiness in the house was the worst. Every corner, every room, every object held a memory, a ghost of her presence. The silence was deafening, broken only by the ticking of the clock, each second a relentless reminder of time marching on, of a life irrevocably altered. The coffee cups remained on the counter, two, always two, a stark visual representation of our shattered unity. Her clothes, still hanging in the closet, seemed to hold her essence, a ghostly fragrance that both comforted and tormented me. Sleep became a battlefield, each night a struggle against nightmares of her illness, her suffering, and the finality of her passing. The recurring imagery, the vivid hallucinations, became an excruciating part of the grieving process, adding a further layer of complexity to the pain.

My anger was a constant companion, a burning ember within the ashes of my grief. Anger at the system, at the alleged negligence that had, I believed, contributed to her suffering and untimely death. Anger at fate, at the injustice of it all. Anger at myself, for not being able to save her, for not being able to stop the inevitable. This anger, initially a consuming force, eventually fueled a determination to seek justice, to ensure that no one else would suffer the same fate. It became a mission, a purpose, a way to channel my grief into something productive, something meaningful.

The spiritual and philosophical perspectives that had provided solace during Connie's illness now offered little comfort. The teachings of Lord Krishna, which had once provided a framework for acceptance, seemed to offer little help in the face of such overwhelming loss. The wisdom of Chanakya, so helpful in navigating life's complexities, felt inadequate in confronting the brutal simplicity of death. The questions were relentless: Why her? Why now? What meaning could possibly be derived from such a devastating loss? My carefully constructed worldview, my carefully cultivated understanding of life and death, lay shattered, replaced by a chaotic jumble of unanswered questions and unbearable sorrow.

In the quiet moments, alone with my memories, I found myself revisiting the myriad details of our life together. The shared laughter during our trip to the Amalfi Coast, the quiet evenings spent reading poetry by the fireplace, the countless conversations about life, death, and the meaning of it all. Each memory became a precious jewel, a fragment of a life that, though gone, remained deeply embedded in my heart. These memories, sharp and clear, were both solace and torment, proof of the love we shared, a constant reminder of what I had lost.

The initial shock had subsided, replaced by a chronic ache, a deep-seated emptiness that refused to be filled. The world felt muted, the colors less vibrant, the sounds less sharp. I was moving through a world drained of color, existing only on the pale edges of my grief. I started to understand the truth of those who had experienced loss – the isolation, the disconnection, the constant sense of being adrift. The practicalities of life continued, but they felt meaningless, disconnected from the core of my being.

The journey of grief is not a linear path. It's a winding, often tortuous road, filled with unexpected twists and turns. There are moments of clarity, followed by waves of crushing sorrow, moments of peace, followed by fits of unyielding anger. There is no timetable, no map to guide the way. It's a journey of navigating the unknown, of finding one's footing in the shifting sands of loss. And even amidst the darkness, there are glimmers of light, moments of unexpected grace, moments of connection that offer a lifeline in the depths of despair. These are the moments that sustain us, that give us the strength to continue, to navigate the treacherous path ahead. The path that, for now, I walk alone, carrying the memory of Connie, my love, my life, my soul mate, forever within my heart.

## Navigating the Initial Shock

The world fractured. One moment, the rhythmic rasp of Connie's breathing, the subtle shift of her hand in mine – anchors in the storm of her illness – the next, a void. A silence so profound it felt like a physical weight pressing down, crushing the air from my lungs. The doctors' words, carefully chosen, professionally delivered, blurred into an incomprehensible drone. "We did everything we could," they said, their faces etched with the weariness of a battle lost. But what did that even mean? What could possibly constitute "everything" in the face of such a devastating loss? The reality of her absence slammed into me with the force of a tidal wave, leaving me gasping for breath, struggling to find purchase in the shifting sands of a life irrevocably altered.

The initial days were a blur, a surreal tapestry woven from fragmented memories and emotional wreckage. Sleep offered no solace, only a descent into a deeper abyss of grief, punctuated by jolts of sudden awareness – the empty space beside me in bed, the silence in the house, the absence of her gentle humming in the kitchen. Each mundane task, once shared, now felt like a leaden weight, a cruel reminder of her absence. The simple act of making coffee, once a shared ritual, became a ritual of mourning, the aroma a phantom echo of her presence. Even the comforting weight of her favorite armchair, usually occupied by her vibrant presence, now felt oppressive, a constant, palpable reminder of what was lost.

My mind, usually a well-ordered landscape of thoughts and strategies, was a chaotic wilderness, overgrown with tangled emotions. Rational thought struggled against a tide of overwhelming sorrow. I found myself staring blankly at walls, unable to process the enormity of what had happened. The world continued its relentless march forward, oblivious to the catastrophic shift in my own reality. Cars honked, birds chirped, life went on, but mine had stopped. Or rather, it felt like it had been hijacked, diverted onto a desolate path leading to an unknown destination.

The outpouring of sympathy, while well-meaning, felt strangely inadequate, a stark contrast to the gaping chasm of my grief. Friends and colleagues offered condolences, platitudes that echoed hollowly in the cavern of my despair. Their words, intended to comfort, served only to highlight the stark reality of my solitude, the crushing loneliness of a life lived without Connie. I would smile, nod, utter the expected responses, but inside, a storm raged, a maelstrom of emotions that threatened to consume me.

My rational mind, honed by years of crisis management, struggled to assert itself. I attempted to construct a narrative, a logical framework to explain what had happened, to impose order on the chaos. But the facts, the cold, hard facts, offered no solace. Connie's death, while preceded by a long and arduous battle with cancer, felt premature, unjust, a violation of the natural order. The anger began to simmer, a slow burn beneath the surface of my grief, fueled by questions that remained unanswered, by suspicions that gnawed at the edges of my consciousness. Had there been medical negligence? Were there opportunities missed? The meticulous, analytical part of my brain began to take over, seeking answers, demanding accountability.

This dual experience – the overwhelming emotional pain and the simmering rage – proved to be a powerful combination. The grief threatened to paralyze me, while the anger fueled a determination to seek justice, to make sense of the senseless. It was a complex dance between despair and defiance, between acceptance and outrage. The sheer intensity of these conflicting emotions was both terrifying and strangely empowering. In the midst of the darkness, it seemed, there were glimmers of a fierce, unwavering resolve.

My professional life, usually a source of comfort and stability, now felt like an alien landscape. The structured routines, the strategic thinking, the calculated responses all seemed futile in the face of my grief. I found myself retreating into myself, my energy sapped, my motivation depleted. Even the familiar challenges I normally relished now seemed insurmountable, their significance diminished by the enormity of my personal loss. The world, once a vibrant tapestry of opportunity and engagement, now felt muted, devoid of color and vitality.

My spiritual and philosophical leanings, usually a source of strength and perspective, offered little consolation in the immediate aftermath. The teachings of Lord Krishna, the wisdom of Chanakya, the comforting words of spiritual texts – all seemed remote, abstract concepts that failed to bridge the gulf between the theoretical and the visceral reality of my loss. The concepts of acceptance, resilience, and the impermanence of life, while intellectually understood, offered little practical comfort in the face of such profound pain. The spiritual tools I had relied upon for years felt inadequate, ineffective against the force of my grief. It was a period of spiritual wrestling, a confrontation with the limitations of even the deepest belief systems.

The physical manifestations of my grief were as profound as the emotional ones. Sleep became a battlefield, a nightly struggle against insomnia and nightmares. My appetite vanished, leaving me gaunt and weak. My once robust health deteriorated, the constant stress triggering physical ailments. Simple tasks that once flowed smoothly now seemed monumental, my energy drained, my body depleted. The mundane routine of daily life, once a source of order and comfort, became a series of grueling challenges. It was a testament to the all-encompassing nature of grief, its ability to infiltrate every aspect of existence, leaving no part of life untouched.

Yet, amidst the overwhelming despair, there were glimmers of light, fragile moments of connection that hinted at the possibility of healing. A kind word from a neighbor, a gentle touch from a friend, a shared memory with a colleague – these small acts of kindness, these unexpected expressions of empathy, served as lifelines in the turbulent sea of grief. They were reminders that I was not alone, that others understood, that the darkness was not absolute. They were the seeds of hope, planted in the fertile ground of my sorrow, awaiting the time for their growth and blossoming. The journey was long, the path fraught with peril, but the possibility of healing, the potential for finding meaning in the face of loss, began to emerge from the depths of my despair. It was a gradual process, a slow and painstaking reconstruction of a shattered world, but it was a process nonetheless. The seeds of resilience were sown, even as the storm raged. The echoes of Connie's laughter, once a vibrant presence, would now become the whispers that guide me through the darkness, a promise of a future where her memory would be a light, rather than a shadow. The journey was long, arduous, but I would walk it, one step at a time, guided by love, justice, and the enduring power of the spirit.

## The Pain of Absence

The house felt cavernous, echoing with the absence that had become its new inhabitant. Every corner, every room, whispered her name – Connie. The scent of her favorite jasmine perfume, a phantom presence lingering stubbornly on the pillows, was a cruel mockery of her absence. The silence, once a comfort, now clawed at my sanity, a constant, gnawing reminder of the void she left behind. It wasn't just her physical absence that tore at me; it was the absence of her laughter, her insightful observations, her gentle hand resting on mine during late-night conversations. The absence of her presence, a presence so profound it felt like a second skin. The routines we shared, meticulously crafted over four decades, now lay in ruins, shards of a broken mirror reflecting a fractured self. Breakfast without her was a lonely ritual, dinner a mournful affair, the settings for two mocking my solitude. Even the mundane tasks, once shared moments of connection, now felt like a constant, agonizing reminder of what was irretrievably lost.

The first few weeks were a blur of numbness, a surreal state where grief existed as a detached observer, not a visceral experience. Then came the sharp, piercing pain – a physical ache that emanated from the deepest recesses of my being. It manifested in a thousand different ways: a tightness in my chest that made breathing difficult, a constant tremor in my hands, an exhaustion that sleep couldn't alleviate. It wasn't merely sadness; it was a profound sense of disorientation, a loss of grounding, a shattering of my very identity. I had spent forty-one years as half of a whole, and now I was irrevocably, painfully incomplete.

The crisis management training I'd undergone over the years provided a framework for dealing with external crises, but it offered little solace against the internal turmoil of bereavement. I could analyze the situation logically, identifying the triggers, anticipating the potential pitfalls, but the emotional onslaught was overwhelming. My rational mind wrestled with the irrationality of grief, its capricious nature, its relentless demands. I found myself clinging to rituals, to routines, as desperate attempts to maintain a semblance of normalcy. But these were hollow gestures, flimsy attempts to fill the vacuum left by Connie's absence.

The silence of the nights was particularly brutal. The gentle rhythm of her breathing, once a lullaby, was replaced by an oppressive silence that amplified the emptiness of the bed. I tried sleeping pills, meditation, even a return to the classical music we both loved, but nothing could quiet the cacophony of memories that flooded my mind as soon as darkness fell. The pain wasn't just emotional; it was profoundly physical. Sleep offered no escape, only a succession of vivid dreams punctuated by nightmarish awakenings. In these dreams, Connie was sometimes near, sometimes far, her image constantly shifting, frustrating my attempts to grasp the ephemeral nature of memory itself. The dreams were disorienting, a disconcerting mix of real and imagined, a surreal landscape where the line between life and death dissolved.

The anger, fueled by my suspicion of medical negligence, only intensified my suffering. The legal battle ahead felt like another layer of pain, a Sisyphean task that promised no true resolution. How could I possibly navigate this labyrinthine system, seeking justice while wrestling with the crushing weight of grief? The anger provided a temporary distraction, a necessary counterpoint to the overwhelming despair, a sense that I could, at least, fight for something, even if that something was a hollow pursuit of accountability for a loss that could never be reversed. It gave me a purpose, however grim, a focus amidst the chaos.

My spiritual beliefs, once a source of comfort, felt distant, obscured by the thick fog of grief. I studied the Bhagavad Gita again, searching for solace in Lord Krishna's words. I reflected on Chanakya's wisdom, seeking an understanding of the impermanence of life. But the profound philosophical concepts felt hollow, distant echoes in the face of such profound personal devastation. The wisdom of ages seemed powerless to alleviate the sharp, immediate pain of my loss. I found myself questioning everything I believed in, grappling with the seeming unfairness of it all. Why her? Why now? These questions, devoid of answers, gnawed at me, exacerbating the already unbearable pain of absence.

The support of friends and family was a lifeline, albeit one that felt insufficient at times. Their well-meaning attempts to console me, while appreciated, often felt inadequate. They spoke of acceptance, of moving on, of finding peace. But acceptance felt like surrender, moving on felt like betrayal, and peace seemed an impossible, distant shore. I appreciated their presence, their gestures of kindness, but I couldn't fully embrace their advice. How could I accept the unacceptable? How could I move on from a life inextricably intertwined with Connie's? How could I find peace when my soul was fractured? Their words, though meant to comfort, often highlighted the magnitude of my loss, the chasm between my world before Connie's passing and my new, desolate reality.

The simple act of going to the grocery store, once a mundane task, became a Herculean effort. Walking down the aisles, surrounded by the clamor of daily life, felt utterly alien. Each mundane purchase seemed a betrayal, a frivolous act in the face of such profound loss. I found myself scrutinizing each item, lingering over familiar products that Connie would have chosen, overwhelmed by the weight of her absence, the poignant reminder of a shared past now irrevocably lost.

Even the simplest conversations felt strained, my words stumbling, my thoughts a jumbled mess of grief and anger. I found myself withdrawing from social interactions, finding solace only in solitude, in the quiet spaces where I could grieve without the pressure of having to appear strong, composed, or even remotely functional. Solitude, once a refuge, had become a prison, its walls lined with the echoes of our shared memories. The memories were precious and painful, beautiful and heartbreaking, constantly reminding me of my irrevocable loss.

The world continued to turn, oblivious to my suffering. People went about their daily lives, their routines undisturbed by the seismic shift that had altered my existence. This seeming indifference only intensified my isolation, fueling my sense of profound disconnect. The world felt callous, heartless, indifferent to my pain. I felt utterly alone in my grief, trapped in a private hell of despair and loneliness. This profound sense of isolation was perhaps the most excruciating aspect of my grief, a deep-seated loneliness that went beyond the simple absence of Connie's physical presence.

Slowly, painstakingly, I began to construct a new reality, a life that would accommodate the profound void she left. It was not a matter of forgetting Connie, but of learning to live with her absence, of integrating her memory into the fabric of my new existence. It was a process of redefining my identity, of accepting the irretrievable loss and finding a path forward. The journey was long, the pain relentless, but the possibility of healing, the glimmer of hope, began to emerge from the depths of my despair. It wasn't a matter of erasing the pain, but of learning to live alongside it, acknowledging its existence, understanding its nature, and finding ways to navigate the complexities of this new reality.

The path ahead would be fraught with challenges, but the love I shared with Connie, the memories we created, the lessons we learned together, would serve as a compass, guiding me through the darkness, towards a future where her memory, while eternally poignant, would also be a source of strength and inspiration. The memories would become my guiding lights, the love our eternal bond. The journey would be long, and there would be many dark days ahead; but I would continue walking. One step at a time. Guided by love, justice, and the enduring power of the human spirit. The pain of absence might forever remain a constant companion, but it would no longer define me. I would find a way to integrate it into the narrative of my life, to transform it from a source of debilitating despair into a catalyst for growth and understanding.

# The Crumbling World

The world, once vibrant and shared, had become a monochrome landscape. The familiar comfort of routine, the bedrock of our forty-one years together, crumbled into dust. Waking up in the morning, the first act was a physical manifestation of loss. The space beside me, once warmed by Connie's presence, felt icy and vast. The sun, once a shared sight, now felt like a cruel spotlight illuminating my solitude. The simple act of making coffee, once a quiet communion, was now a bitter ritual, each drop a reminder of the shared mornings that were no more.

The house, once our sanctuary, now felt like a mausoleum. Every object held a memory, each memory a dagger twisting in my heart. Her favorite armchair, empty and waiting; her books, untouched, their pages whispering forgotten stories; her paintings, vibrant and beautiful, yet infused with a haunting silence that reflected the emptiness within me. Even the garden, once our shared haven, where we spent countless hours tending to roses and discussing philosophy under the shade of the old oak tree, felt desolate and unkempt, mirroring the state of my soul.

Practical tasks that were once effortlessly shared now loomed as insurmountable mountains. Paying bills, managing finances, even simple household chores felt impossible. Connie had handled so much of it, her efficiency and organizational skills a constant source of support. Now, every mundane decision felt weighted down by the gravity of her absence. The bureaucratic maze of insurance claims, legal matters related to her estate, became battles I fought alone, each phone call, each document a fresh wound. The world, designed for two, now demanded I navigate it alone, stripped of the support system we had meticulously built together.

Social interactions, once a source of joy and connection, became excruciating. Friends' well-meaning inquiries felt like intrusions, their attempts at comfort falling flat, their words echoing in the void of my understanding. Their sympathetic glances felt like accusations of inadequacy. I found myself avoiding social gatherings, retreating into the shell of my grief, unable to face the world without her. The vibrant tapestry of our social life, woven with threads of shared friendships and intellectual discussions, unraveled, leaving behind only frayed edges. Silence became my only companion, a deafening silence punctuated only by the echoes of memories and the incessant throbbing of my grief.

The anger, a raw, consuming fire, raged within me, adding another layer of complexity to my suffering. The medical negligence, the missed diagnoses, the series of unfortunate events that culminated in Connie's untimely death, fueled a fire of righteous indignation. My attempts to seek justice, to hold those responsible accountable, became another consuming battle fought amidst the wreckage of my grief. Each legal hurdle, each bureaucratic obstacle, only served to intensify my anger, to sharpen the edge of my pain. It felt like a war waged on multiple fronts, the battle against grief intertwined with the struggle for justice.

My spiritual practices, once a source of solace and strength, seemed to offer little comfort. The philosophical concepts I had studied with Connie, the teachings of Lord Krishna on dharma and karma, the wisdom of Chanakya on justice and strategy, seemed distant, abstract. The profound truths that once resonated with me now felt hollow and empty. The serenity I had once found in meditation was replaced by an agonizing restlessness, my mind a tempestuous sea of sorrow. The very acts of prayer felt like a futile exercise, my pleas unheard, my grief unanswered.

Sleep became a battlefield, a place where dreams and nightmares battled for dominance. I was haunted by vivid images of Connie, her face pale and weakened by illness, her eyes reflecting a mixture of pain and resignation. I would wake up in a cold sweat, the phantom touch of her hand lingering on mine, only to realize that it was but a cruel trick of memory and grief. Even the tranquility of slumber was hijacked by loss, a stark reminder of the vast chasm that had opened up in my life.

The simplest of actions, once seamless and effortless, became herculean tasks. Even eating became a chore, each bite a tasteless reminder of our shared meals, the laughter and conversations that once accompanied them. The joy of savoring food, the pleasure of shared moments, was lost in the desolate landscape of my grief. The very act of living felt like an endurance test, each day a marathon run through a desert of sorrow.

My identity, once intricately interwoven with Connie's, felt fragmented, shattered. I struggled to define myself beyond the role of "Connie's husband," a label that had become so deeply ingrained in my being. Who was I without her? What were my passions, my aspirations, my goals, now that the life we had meticulously crafted together lay in ruins? The question hung heavy in the air, a profound void in the fabric of my selfhood. My world, built on a foundation of shared dreams, purpose, and love, had imploded, leaving behind a void that seemed bottomless.

The healing process felt like an endless climb up a steep, unforgiving mountain. Each step was arduous, each victory fleeting. The path was uncertain, the terrain treacherous, and the summit seemed impossibly far. Yet, within the heart of the storm, a small flame of hope flickered. The love I shared with Connie, the memories we created, the lessons we learned together, served as beacons in the darkness, providing a glimmer of light to guide me through the labyrinth of my grief. It was a long, winding path, full of pain and hardship, but I walked on, one step at a time, my heart heavy, yet fueled by the enduring power of love, and the burning desire for justice. The memory of her laughter, the warmth of her love, the quiet strength of her spirit, these would be my guiding lights, illuminating the path towards a future where her memory, eternally poignant, would also be a source of strength and inspiration.

## Seeking Solace in Reflection

The initial shock gave way to a numbness so profound it felt like a second death. The world continued its relentless spin, oblivious to the gaping chasm ripped through my existence. Days blurred into weeks, each indistinguishable from the last, a monotonous procession of empty moments punctuated by the echoing silence of our home. Sleep offered no respite, only a fleeting escape into dreams haunted by Connie's fading image, her weakened smile, her labored breaths. Food held no appeal; each bite a painful reminder of the meals we'd shared, the laughter that once accompanied them. The simple act of breathing felt like a Herculean task, each inhalation a sharp stab of grief, each exhalation a sigh of resigned despair.

My coping mechanisms were as varied as they were ineffective. Initially, I threw myself into work, the demanding nature of crisis management a temporary anesthetic. The adrenaline rush of resolving complex situations provided a fleeting distraction, a momentary escape from the crushing weight of my loss. But the respite was short-lived. The silence of the evening would return with brutal force, shattering the fragile façade I'd constructed.

I tried to fill the void with mindless activities – long walks, aimless drives, endless hours spent tending to the garden Connie loved so dearly. Each activity was a desperate attempt to occupy my mind, to silence the incessant whispers of grief that haunted my every waking moment. Yet, these actions felt hollow, futile attempts to outrun a shadow that clung to me relentlessly.

Friends and family offered comfort, their presence a lifeline in a sea of despair. Their words, though well-meaning, often fell flat, their inability to comprehend the depth of my suffering adding another layer of isolation. Their attempts to cheer me, to distract me, felt like intrusions into a sacred space of mourning, a place where I needed to grapple with my pain in solitude. Yet, I knew their intentions were pure, their concern genuine, and I clung to their support, however inadequate it may have felt.

I found solace, unexpectedly, in spirituality. The philosophical frameworks I'd explored throughout my life – the teachings of Krishna, the strategic wisdom of Chanakya, the contemplative serenity of Buddhist thought – offered a new lens through which to view my grief. Their insights into the cyclical nature of life and death, the impermanence of all things, offered a glimmer of understanding, a sense of perspective in the face of my profound loss.

The Bhagavad Gita, with its exploration of dharma and karma, provided a framework for understanding my grief as part of a larger cosmic order. Krishna's words, "Perform your duty without attachment to the fruits of your actions," resonated deeply. My duty, I realized, was not to escape grief, but to process it, to learn from it, to find a way to honor Connie's memory and integrate her absence into the fabric of my life.

Chanakya's teachings on strategic thinking, though seemingly distant from the realm of personal grief, offered a surprising sense of structure. His emphasis on clarity, analysis, and decisive action resonated with my need to navigate the complex emotions of bereavement. I began to approach my grief not as a chaotic storm, but as a challenge that required careful strategizing, a battle I could wage with purpose and determination. Each tear was a data point, each sleepless night a moment for introspection, each outburst of anger a fuel for change.

Buddhist philosophy, with its emphasis on acceptance and impermanence, proved particularly helpful in this phase. The concept of *anicca* – the understanding that everything is in constant flux – reminded me that my pain, like all things, was temporary. It was not a permanent condition, but a phase I would eventually traverse, albeit painfully. The acceptance of this reality, however challenging, provided a subtle shift in perspective, a crack of light in the suffocating darkness.

But my grief was not solely a spiritual journey; it was intertwined with a profound sense of injustice. The alleged medical negligence that contributed to Connie's death fueled a burning rage within me. This anger, initially overwhelming, eventually became a driving force, transforming my grief into a quest for justice. The process of seeking accountability, of confronting those responsible for Connie's suffering, became a necessary component of my healing process. It was a fight not just for justice, but for Connie's legacy, a way to ensure her memory wouldn't be tarnished by the careless indifference of others.

The fight for justice was arduous. Navigating the labyrinthine corridors of the legal system demanded resilience, patience, and a relentless determination. Each step forward was often followed by two steps back. Yet, the fight provided a structure, a purpose, in the midst of my despair. It was an outlet for my anger, a channel for my grief. It was a way to transform my pain into action, to channel my sorrow into a purpose beyond myself. And it served as a stark reminder of the moral and ethical failures that lay beyond the bounds of personal loss.

The initial months were a battle for survival. I clung to routine, to the remnants of our shared life. The house, once filled with laughter and the aroma of Connie's cooking, now echoed with silence, a monument to our love and loss. I would wander through the rooms, touching her belongings, breathing in the faint scent of her perfume, trying to hold on to the vestiges of her presence. Each object was a memory, each memory a fresh wound.

My writing became a form of therapy, a way to process my grief and give voice to my pain. The act of recording my memories, of articulating my feelings, allowed me to confront the depths of my sorrow, to transform the formless chaos of grief into a narrative, a story I could share and understand.

The process of writing this book has been a profound journey, a harrowing yet cathartic exploration of loss, love, and the complexities of grief. It has been a path paved with tears, anger, and moments of profound despair. Yet, within this journey, I have discovered a strength I never knew I possessed, a resilience forged in the crucible of loss. I have found solace in reflection, in the wisdom of spiritual teachings, and in the pursuit of justice. Through this process, I have begun to understand that grief is not a linear process, but a winding path, full of setbacks and breakthroughs, of darkness and light. And I have come to realize that the love I shared with Connie, the memories we created together, and the lessons we learned from each other, remain as powerful and vibrant as ever, shaping who I am, even in the face of this profound and enduring loss.

The emptiness continues, but it's now tinged with a different color, a quieter sadness perhaps, a more accepting melancholy. It's the sadness of a man who knows his heart will forever hold a space for the woman he loved, a space that will never be truly filled, but a space where love and memory reside, eternally intertwined. This is where I find solace; not in an absence of pain, but in the acceptance of its enduring presence. The journey continues, and this journey, though still marked by sorrow, is one now punctuated by hope. A hope ignited by the enduring power of love, the memory of Connie, and the unwavering pursuit of justice. And with that, a new phase in my life emerges, a life that though forever changed, still pulses with the echoes of a love that transcends even death itself. The path ahead remains uncertain, but the footsteps I take are now infused with a determination born from both my grief and my enduring love for Connie. This book is a testament to that. It is a tribute to a love story, a journey of grief, and an ongoing pursuit of justice. The journey is far from over, but the path, once obscured by grief, is now slightly clearer, illuminated by love, memory, and the steadfast pursuit of a justice that remains a deeply personal, yet essential, part of my healing.

## Allegations of Medical Negligence

The initial shock of Connie's passing gave way to a chilling realization: something felt profoundly wrong. The aggressive nature of her cancer's progression, the seemingly rushed decisions made during her treatment, and the lack of thorough explanations from her medical team – these elements coalesced into a growing suspicion. It wasn't simply grief that consumed me; it was a simmering anger, fueled by a deep-seated feeling of injustice. My background in crisis management, accustomed to analyzing situations with a cool head, now found itself grappling with a personal crisis of immense proportions. My rational mind, trained to assess risks and mitigate damage, struggled to accept the narrative presented to me. Connie's death, I increasingly felt, wasn't merely the tragic result of a relentless disease; there were indications that medical negligence played a significant role.

The seeds of this conviction were sown in the final weeks of Connie's life. The rapid decline in her condition, after a period of apparent stability, seemed inconsistent with the assurances we'd received from her oncologist. Several critical decisions, such as the timing of aggressive interventions and the choice of specific treatments, appeared rushed and lacked the thorough explanation and exploration of alternatives I would have expected given my own professional experience in risk assessment. There were instances where communication broke down, leaving us feeling bewildered and uninformed during crucial moments. The sense of being rushed, the lack of detailed explanations, the feeling of being treated as just another case – all of these combined to fuel my suspicion that something wasn't right.

My initial inquiries were met with vague reassurances and a dismissive tone. The medical team seemed more focused on adhering to protocols than engaging in a genuine dialogue about Connie's care. This further solidified my resolve to investigate further. My grief was a powerful motivator, but it wasn't the only driver. My sense of justice, honed by years of navigating complex situations and advocating for fairness, demanded a deeper examination. I felt a moral obligation to understand what happened, not just for my own peace of mind, but to ensure that no one else would suffer the same fate.

This pursuit of justice wasn't a simplistic quest for vengeance. It was a complex endeavor, fraught with emotional turmoil and procedural hurdles. My training in crisis management proved unexpectedly valuable, equipping me with the skills to gather information systematically, analyze data objectively, and formulate a coherent narrative. I meticulously reviewed Connie's medical records, gathering every piece of documentation, every test result, every doctor's note. I sought second opinions from independent oncologists, presenting them with the complete medical history and asking for their expert assessments.

The responses I received confirmed my worst fears. Several independent experts pointed to significant deviations from standard medical practices in Connie's treatment. They highlighted instances of inadequate monitoring, delayed intervention, and a lack of informed consent regarding certain procedures. Their findings provided a concrete basis for my burgeoning suspicion that medical negligence played a crucial role in accelerating Connie's decline and ultimately contributing to her untimely death. The reports were detailed, citing specific examples and referencing established medical guidelines. These reports, armed with expert opinions, became the foundation of my efforts to pursue accountability.

The legal process proved to be a formidable challenge. Navigating the intricacies of medical malpractice litigation was a steep learning curve. The jargon, the technicalities, the sheer volume of paperwork – it was an overwhelming experience. Moreover, the emotional toll was immense. Each legal filing, each deposition, each courtroom encounter, was a painful reminder of my loss and the injustice I was fighting against. Yet, the conviction that fueled my pursuit of justice remained unshaken. The anger, initially a consuming force, began to transform into a resolute determination.

The initial stages of the legal battle focused on gathering evidence and building a strong case. This involved painstakingly compiling medical records, securing expert testimony, and meticulously documenting every step of the process. The fight for accountability wasn't merely a personal endeavor; it became a commitment to a broader cause – the protection of patients' rights and the prevention of future medical negligence. It became a quest to ensure transparency and accountability within the healthcare system. The experiences along this path were both disheartening and inspiring. The initial setbacks were frustrating, but the unwavering support from a few key individuals – my family, close friends, and a few exceptionally dedicated lawyers – kept me going.

I faced significant opposition from the medical establishment. There were attempts to dismiss my claims, to downplay the severity of the negligence, and to portray me as an emotionally distraught individual incapable of objective judgment. However, the strength of the medical experts' reports and my own meticulous documentation allowed me to counter these assertions. I learned to leverage my crisis management skills to effectively communicate my case, to present the evidence logically and persuasively, and to maintain a composed demeanor even in the face of intense pressure.

This journey wasn't just about legal victory; it was about finding a measure of closure. It was about understanding the sequence of events that led to Connie's death, and holding those responsible accountable. It was about ensuring that the lessons learned from this tragedy would prevent similar occurrences in the future. Although I'm still navigating this emotional landscape, there's a strange sense of satisfaction in knowing that I've done everything in my power to bring justice to Connie's memory. The battle continues, but the fight has already transformed into a mission to ensure that no one else faces similar medical negligence and loss.

The legal proceedings also became a catalyst for personal growth. The ordeal forced me to confront my own vulnerabilities and limitations, to acknowledge the depth of my grief and anger, and to find healthy ways to process those emotions. I engaged in therapy, found solace in meditation, and reconnected with my spiritual beliefs, drawing strength from the wisdom of Lord Krishna and Chanakya, whose teachings on acceptance and justice provided guidance during this difficult period. Their philosophies, particularly Krishna's teachings on accepting what cannot be changed and Chanakya's emphasis on the importance of dharma and justice, helped me navigate the complexities of grief, anger, and the arduous path toward justice.

The process challenged my understanding of justice itself. It wasn't simply about winning a legal battle; it was about seeking truth and accountability, about ensuring that those responsible for medical negligence would be held accountable for their actions. It was about using my experience and skills to advocate for a more just and transparent healthcare system. It was also a deep personal quest for understanding, a desperate search for answers that might never fully satisfy. The pursuit of justice, interwoven with the overwhelming grief, has been a crucible forging a new identity – one marked by both pain and a steely determination to fight for what's right. This fight, though born from tragedy, has become a testament to Connie's memory, her indomitable spirit and our enduring love. The fight for justice is an ongoing testament to the power of love in the face of overwhelming loss and the importance of holding those accountable for their actions. It's a tribute to Connie, and a warning to those who might neglect their duty of care. The fight continues, not just for closure, but for a better world where such negligence is minimized and justice prevails.

# The Fight for Accountability

The initial stages of my pursuit felt surreal. Filing the complaint, a stark, official document detailing the perceived medical failings that contributed to Connie's death, felt like a betrayal of the quiet intimacy of our life together. It was a jarring transition from the hushed grief of her memorial service to the stark reality of the legal arena. The methodical compilation of medical records, each page a stark reminder of her suffering, was a painstaking process, a descent into the clinical details that overshadowed the vibrant woman they described. I meticulously gathered every document: appointment schedules, lab results, notes from consultations, even discharge summaries – each one a piece of the puzzle I was desperately trying to assemble. The sheer volume of information was overwhelming at times, a testament to the complexity of her care and the subsequent difficulty in dissecting it for potential negligence.

My professional experience in crisis management proved invaluable. I approached the task with a methodical, almost detached precision, creating a detailed chronology of Connie's illness, highlighting the points of concern. I identified patterns, inconsistencies, and potential lapses in judgment. My background, normally employed in analyzing corporate crises, now served as a tool to dissect this personal tragedy, converting raw emotion into a structured argument. The process was agonizing, a constant oscillation between the searing pain of my loss and the cold logic of legal procedure. Every detail, every date, every medical term, was a painful reminder of Connie's fading strength. Yet, within that pain, a quiet determination hardened. I was not just a grieving husband; I was a pursuer of justice.

The legal process itself was a labyrinthine journey. Navigating the complexities of medical malpractice claims required patience, persistence, and an unwavering commitment. I consulted with lawyers specializing in medical negligence, enduring countless hours of consultations, poring over legal precedents, and absorbing complex medical terminology. The initial consultations were daunting. Lawyers, with their professional detachment, approached the situation with meticulous analysis, dissecting the medical records with a clinical precision that sometimes felt insensitive. Their questions, aimed at establishing a solid case, often reopened fresh wounds, forcing me to relive the anguish of Connie's final days.

The initial assessment itself involved a lengthy and agonizing review of the medical records. Experts were consulted – oncologists, radiologists, and other specialists – each offering their analysis of the treatment provided to Connie. Their reports were critical, some identifying potential areas of negligence, others expressing caution, citing the inherent uncertainties of cancer treatment. This process, while critical to building a case, felt deeply frustrating. The uncertainty was agonizing, the wait for their opinions excruciating. Meanwhile, my grief was a relentless companion, a heavy shroud that seemed to accompany me in every meeting, in every phone call.

The emotional toll was immense. The legal fight, while necessary, was a battle fought on a battlefield of sorrow. Every court document, every legal filing, was a constant reminder of Connie's absence. Sleep became a luxury, replaced by nightmares of the hospital corridors and the antiseptic scent that forever clung to my memories. Friends offered support, but their attempts to provide solace often felt inadequate. How could anyone truly understand the depth of my pain, the searing absence that had hollowed out my life? My own professional experience in managing crises offered little comfort. This was a crisis of a different order of magnitude, a personal catastrophe that defied rational analysis.

The initial response from the medical institution was a carefully constructed wall of professional jargon and legal obfuscation. Their lawyers engaged in a slow, deliberate strategy designed to wear me down, to delay and deflect. It felt like a system designed to protect itself at the expense of truth and justice. The bureaucratic maze added insult to injury, the impersonal nature of the legal battle further compounding my already immense emotional distress. Each delayed response, each evasive answer, fueled my anger and strengthened my resolve.

The fight was far from over. The pursuit of justice wasn't about revenge; it wasn't about monetary compensation, though that would undeniably be part of the process. It was about accountability. It was about ensuring that no other family would have to endure the pain and uncertainty that we had faced. It was about demanding transparency and responsibility from those entrusted with the care of others. The legal fight became a proxy for the profound grief I carried. Each step forward, however small, was a testament to Connie's life and a blow against the indifference that nearly silenced her voice.

The emotional cost was high. There were days when the weight of grief threatened to overwhelm me. I relied on spiritual practices, meditation and prayer, to find moments of solace amidst the storm. The wisdom of Lord Krishna, which Connie and I had often discussed, provided a framework for understanding suffering and finding inner peace. The teachings of Chanakya, with his emphasis on justice and duty, further fueled my determination to fight for what I believed was right.

However, beyond the spiritual guidance, the support of my friends and family was invaluable. They listened patiently, often silently, offering a shoulder to cry on, a comforting presence in the face of my despair. Their empathy, their understanding, and their unwavering support proved to be the anchors that kept me from drifting entirely adrift in the sea of my grief. They understood that my pursuit of justice was not just about legal proceedings; it was about honoring Connie's memory, about fighting for the dignity she deserved, even in death.

The legal battles stretched over several years, punctuated by court appearances, depositions, and countless hours spent reviewing and analyzing evidence. Each stage felt like a fresh wound, forcing me to relive the trauma. The legal system, while designed to deliver justice, often felt cumbersome and frustrating. But, with every hurdle overcome, my resolve grew stronger.

The fight for accountability became a personal pilgrimage, a path forged in sorrow but leading towards a fragile sense of healing. It was a testament to the enduring power of love, a love that transcended death and fueled my determination to seek justice, even in the face of seemingly insurmountable odds. It was about more than just Connie's case; it was about the larger system, the need for greater transparency, and the importance of holding those responsible for medical negligence to account. The fight was – and continues to be – a fight for a fairer world, a world where the sanctity of human life is upheld, and where the grief of loss is tempered by the pursuit of justice. The pursuit of justice, interwoven with the enduring power of my love for Connie, became a sacred duty, a testament to our enduring bond – two bodies, one soul, forever connected, even in this struggle.

## Confronting the System

The initial stages of navigating the legal system were disorienting, a stark contrast to the quiet intimacy of my life with Connie. The sterile environment of law offices, the precise language of legal documents, the detached demeanor of some professionals – all felt jarringly at odds with the visceral grief I carried. It was a relentless process, requiring a level of meticulous attention to detail that seemed almost sacrilegious given the personal nature of the information I was handling. Each medical record, each consultation note, was a fresh wound, reopening the pain of Connie's suffering. I found myself poring over these documents for hours, days, weeks, piecing together a narrative of her illness and treatment, searching for evidence of negligence, of missed opportunities, of systemic failures.

The sheer volume of information was staggering. The medical records alone filled several large binders, a testament to the complexity of Connie's advanced cancer and the multifaceted nature of her treatment. I learned to decipher the medical jargon, to understand the nuances of treatment protocols, to identify potential discrepancies in her care. It was a crash course in oncology, pathology, and medical ethics, an unwelcome education I had never anticipated undergoing. Initially, I relied on the support of a legal team, but I quickly realized that I had to become my own advocate. I needed to understand every detail, every nuance, to ensure that Connie's story was accurately and effectively presented.

The process was not without its emotional tolls. There were moments when the sheer weight of the legal battle threatened to overwhelm me. The bureaucratic hurdles were numerous, the delays infuriating. There were times when I questioned whether the fight was even worth it. The emotional labor involved in meticulously documenting Connie's illness and death was immense. The fight for justice felt less like a legal battle and more like a personal pilgrimage, a journey through a landscape of grief and frustration. Sleepless nights were spent reading and rereading documents, cross-referencing dates and times, trying to make sense of a chaotic and ultimately tragic sequence of events.

The frustration intensified as I encountered the cold, impersonal nature of the system. The impersonal nature of dealing with insurance companies, hospital administrators, and medical professionals often left me feeling powerless. They seemed more concerned with procedures and liability than with Connie's suffering and the potential for systemic failure. I found myself grappling with a deep sense of injustice, not only for Connie, but for countless others who had experienced similar situations. The focus on legal technicalities, on the precise wording of forms and documents, felt at times a callous disregard for the human cost of medical negligence.

I also encountered a chilling sense of indifference from some medical professionals. Some were defensive, others dismissive. There were instances where I felt that information was being withheld, or that efforts were being made to minimize the extent of the mistakes that had been made. This only further fueled my determination to fight for accountability. I understood that the fight wasn't just about achieving a specific legal outcome, but about raising awareness, about pushing for systemic change to prevent similar tragedies in the future.

My experiences weren't unique. In conversations with other grieving families, I learned that their journeys were often fraught with similar challenges. The legal system, designed to provide justice and accountability, sometimes felt like an obstacle course, designed to exhaust and discourage those seeking redress. The emotional and financial burdens of legal battles, compounded by the profound grief of losing a loved one, could be insurmountable. I was fortunate to have the resources and support to navigate this process. But many others lacked such resources, leaving them feeling vulnerable and alone in their fight.

The spiritual and philosophical aspects of my life became central to my ability to endure this arduous process. The teachings of Lord Krishna, particularly his emphasis on dharma (duty) and karma (action), provided a framework for understanding my actions. The pursuit of justice wasn't just about retribution; it was about fulfilling my duty to Connie, to ensure that her suffering wasn't in vain. Chanakya's wisdom on the importance of strategy and perseverance proved invaluable in navigating the complexities of the legal system. His teachings reinforced the necessity of patience, of meticulous planning, and of recognizing the strengths and weaknesses of opponents.

My faith provided solace amidst the turmoil. Prayer and meditation helped me to manage the overwhelming emotions and to find moments of peace amidst the chaos. It allowed me to focus on Connie's memory, on the love we shared, rather than allowing myself to be consumed by anger and resentment. There were days when I felt completely drained, emotionally and spiritually depleted. But the memory of Connie, our shared life, the love that bound us, gave me strength to continue. I found solace in shared memories, in revisiting our cherished moments together, reminding myself of the richness and depth of our lives. This emotional sustenance fueled my determination to seek justice, not for personal gratification, but for the greater good.

The fight for justice became a crucible, refining my resolve and deepening my understanding of human nature and the flaws within systems designed to protect us. It was a process of self-discovery, of confronting not only the injustices inflicted upon Connie, but also my own internal struggles with grief, anger, and despair. The pursuit of justice was not merely a legal endeavor; it became a spiritual and philosophical journey, a testament to the enduring power of love and the unwavering commitment to truth and justice, even in the face of seemingly insurmountable odds. My determination was tempered by a profound respect for the system's inherent complexities, yet fueled by an unshakeable belief in the importance of transparency and accountability in the medical profession.

The experience also highlighted the inequities within the healthcare system. Access to quality healthcare is not equally distributed. The cost of medical care is prohibitive for many, leading to compromised care and delayed treatment. This disparity is amplified in cases of serious illness, often leading to devastating consequences. The pursuit of justice for Connie became interwoven with a broader commitment to healthcare reform and advocacy. My journey transformed into a call for transparency and accountability, not just within the specific medical institutions involved, but within the healthcare system as a whole.

The anger I felt was not merely a personal emotion; it was a catalyst for action. It spurred me to delve deeper into the complexities of medical malpractice, the systemic failures that allowed such negligence to occur, and the disproportionate impact on vulnerable populations. This exploration broadened my understanding of the issues at stake, reinforcing my commitment to achieving meaningful change. My experiences underscore the urgent need for greater transparency, improved communication between medical professionals and patients, and stricter accountability measures to prevent similar tragedies in the future.

My journey transformed from a personal struggle for justice into a broader advocacy for systemic change. I understood that Connie's case wasn't isolated; it represented a pattern of medical negligence and the systemic failures that facilitated such injustices. My commitment to justice evolved from a deeply personal grief into a call for meaningful reforms within the healthcare system. The fight wasn't only about holding individuals accountable, but also about transforming the system to prevent future tragedies.

The experience taught me the importance of resilience and perseverance. The legal process was arduous, filled with unexpected setbacks and delays. There were moments of doubt, of questioning whether the fight was worth the emotional toll. But the love for Connie, and the commitment to justice, fueled my determination to continue. The journey underscored the importance of self-care, both physical and mental, in navigating a prolonged crisis.

Ultimately, the pursuit of justice offered a form of catharsis. It wasn't about achieving a complete sense of closure or erasing the pain of loss. But it provided a framework for processing my grief, a channel for channeling my anger into productive action. The journey allowed me to honor Connie's memory, to give voice to her suffering, and to advocate for a better world where healthcare is more equitable, transparent, and accountable. The fight remains ongoing, a testament to the enduring power of love, grief, and the pursuit of justice, a legacy that continues to shape my life. It is a fight not just for Connie, but for all those who have suffered similar losses and for a future where such tragedies are less likely to occur.

The pursuit of justice is a testament to our shared humanity,
a beacon of hope in the face of adversity. And that, in itself,
is a form of healing.

## The Moral Imperative

My anger, initially a raw, consuming fire, began to evolve. It was no longer simply a personal pain, a desperate cry against the unfairness of Connie's passing. It broadened, encompassing a sense of responsibility, a moral imperative that transcended my own grief. Connie's suffering wasn't isolated; it reflected a larger systemic issue, a failure within the healthcare system that allowed negligence to flourish. Her story became a symbol, a representation of countless others who had been similarly wronged, their voices silenced by the complexities of the medical establishment and the chilling indifference of some within it. This realization fueled my resolve, transforming my personal quest for justice into a commitment to broader systemic reform.

The legal battle, though arduous, was not simply about winning a case or securing financial compensation. It was about holding those accountable for their failures, demanding transparency, and ultimately, preventing similar tragedies from occurring. The meticulous gathering of evidence, the countless hours spent scrutinizing medical records, the often-frustrating interactions with legal professionals – these were all acts of defiance against the forces that had contributed to Connie's death. Each step forward felt like a small victory, a chipping away at the formidable wall of bureaucratic indifference.

The process forced me to confront the harsh realities of medical negligence. It wasn't always about malicious intent; often, it stemmed from systemic flaws, inadequate training, overworked staff, and a culture that prioritizes efficiency over individual patient care. I encountered numerous stories from other grieving families, each a mirror reflecting

Connie's suffering. Their shared pain created a powerful sense of solidarity, reinforcing the conviction that my pursuit of justice was not merely a personal vendetta but a fight for a more just and equitable healthcare system.

The moral imperative was deeply intertwined with my spiritual beliefs. My understanding of dharma, the righteous conduct prescribed in Hindu philosophy, guided my actions. The concept of karma, the principle of cause and effect, reinforced the need for accountability. Those who had acted negligently had to bear the consequences of their actions, not just for the sake of retribution, but for the sake of restoring balance and preventing future harm. This wasn't about vengeance; it was about justice, a cornerstone of a moral society.

The writings of Chanakya, the ancient Indian strategist and philosopher, resonated deeply during this period. His emphasis on justice and good governance provided a framework for understanding the systemic failures that had led to Connie's death. His teachings on the importance of ethical leadership and accountability highlighted the need for transparency and reform within the healthcare system. His insights into human nature, particularly the potential for greed and self-interest to corrupt even the noblest institutions, sharpened my understanding of the challenges I faced.

The pursuit of justice was also a deeply personal act of remembrance. It was a way of honoring Connie's life, giving voice to her suffering, and ensuring that her experience wasn't in vain. It was a testament to the depth of our love, a way of keeping her memory alive, not in sorrow alone, but in action. The fight became a continuation of our shared life, a reflection of our commitment to truth, justice, and compassion. It was a way of ensuring that her legacy would not be defined by the tragedy of her untimely death, but by the positive change it sparked.

My experience has revealed a profound disparity between the idealized image of the medical profession and the harsh realities of its everyday functioning. The compassionate healers depicted in literature and media are often at odds with the bureaucratic structures and pressures that can compromise patient care. While many healthcare professionals are dedicated and ethical, the systemic issues I uncovered raise serious concerns about the balance between patient well-being and institutional priorities.

The pursuit of justice often involves navigating a complex maze of legal procedures and bureaucratic hurdles. The language of the law, at times, felt like a foreign language, filled with technical terms and legal jargon. The detachment displayed by some professionals can be jarring, especially for those who are grieving and emotionally vulnerable. The sheer volume of paperwork and the meticulous attention to detail required can be overwhelming, demanding a level of fortitude and organization that feels at odds with the emotional turmoil of loss.

Yet, amidst the challenges, there were moments of unexpected grace. I encountered compassionate lawyers and healthcare professionals who empathized with my situation and worked tirelessly to support my case. The solidarity I found with other grieving families provided a source of strength and resilience. These experiences reinforced my belief in the power of human connection and the importance of empathy in the face of adversity.

Beyond the legal battle, my quest for justice extended to advocating for systemic change within the healthcare industry. I shared Connie's story with various organizations, aiming to raise awareness about the pervasive nature of medical negligence and the need for greater accountability. I believe that transparency and ethical conduct are paramount in healthcare, and that patients have a right to expect high standards of care and accurate information.

My aim wasn't merely to achieve a personal victory in court; it was to contribute to a broader movement for reform. I wanted to create a ripple effect, ensuring that others wouldn't suffer the same fate as Connie. This meant engaging in public advocacy, advocating for policy changes, and supporting organizations dedicated to improving patient safety and accountability within the healthcare system.

The journey of pursuing justice has been a transformative experience, forcing me to confront not only my grief but also the complexities of the healthcare system and the larger societal issues that contribute to medical negligence. It has been a journey of pain, frustration, and anger, but also of hope, resilience, and a renewed sense of purpose. It has been a testament to the enduring power of love and the unwavering commitment to justice, even in the face of unimaginable loss.

This pursuit of justice has also deepened my understanding of the intricate interplay between personal grief and systemic issues. It's not simply about individual failures; it's about the systemic flaws that enable and perpetuate such failures. The pursuit of justice, therefore, involves addressing both the individual accountability and the systemic reforms needed to prevent future tragedies. It requires a multi-pronged approach, engaging with legal avenues, advocating for policy changes, and raising public awareness.

The fight for justice extends beyond the courtroom; it's a fight for systemic change, for a world where healthcare prioritizes patient safety and well-being above all else. It requires a shift in cultural norms and a commitment to transparency and ethical conduct within the healthcare industry. The ultimate goal is not just to achieve retribution for past wrongs but to create a future where such tragedies are less likely to occur. It's a testament to the enduring strength of human spirit and the relentless pursuit of a better world, a world where the loss of a loved one, though deeply painful, is not compounded by the injustice of negligence and indifference. This is a legacy I am committed to building in Connie's memory. It is a testament to the love we shared and a hope for a future where the pursuit of justice is not a battle waged in isolation, but a collective effort to build a healthier, safer, and more equitable world for all. This, more than anything, is my true act of remembrance. It is a gift I give not only to Connie but to all those who have suffered similarly and to those who will come after us.

# The Search for Closure

The legal battle, though arduous and emotionally draining, was ultimately a necessary step. It wasn't solely about retribution, although the desire for accountability was undeniably strong. It was about understanding, about piecing together the fragmented narrative of Connie's final days, seeking answers to the questions that haunted me, the "whys" that echoed in the silence of our empty home. The legal process, with its meticulous documentation and relentless scrutiny, became a form of excavation, unearthing not just the failings of the medical system, but also the hidden cracks in my own understanding of what had transpired.

The depositions, the cross-examinations, the mountains of medical records – they were more than just legal tools; they were instruments of truth-seeking. Each piece of evidence, each testimony, chipped away at the numbness, revealing layers of negligence, miscommunication, and, yes, even indifference. It wasn't a single catastrophic event that led to Connie's death, but a confluence of smaller failures, each seemingly insignificant in isolation, yet cumulatively devastating in their impact. These were not malicious acts, necessarily, but rather a systemic failure to prioritize patient care, a prioritizing of profit over people, an insidious erosion of ethical standards. This realization, while painful, was also cathartic. It allowed me to shift my focus from the abstract notion of injustice to a concrete understanding of the systemic weaknesses that had allowed it to flourish.

The courtroom itself became a strange crucible, a space where grief and anger collided with the detached formality of the legal process. It was a space of profound vulnerability and unexpected resilience. I found myself standing before judges and juries, articulating not only the facts of Connie's case but also the depth of my loss, the irreplaceable void her absence had left in my life. It was an act of raw, unfiltered emotion, a visceral outpouring of grief laid bare under the clinical gaze of the legal system. And yet, paradoxically, this very vulnerability became a source of strength. The act of bearing witness, of sharing Connie's story, transformed my grief from a private anguish into a shared experience, forging unexpected connections with others who understood the depth of my pain.

The outcome of the legal case, while not entirely satisfactory, provided a measure of closure. It wasn't the complete vindication I had initially hoped for, but it brought a sense of accountability, a recognition of the wrongs that had been committed. More importantly, it fueled my resolve to work towards systemic change, to prevent similar tragedies from occurring in the future. The fight for justice had become a mission, a legacy to build in Connie's memory.

Beyond the courtroom battles, the search for closure extended into the realm of spirituality and philosophy. The teachings of Lord Krishna, which Connie and I had often discussed, provided a framework for understanding the impermanence of life and the acceptance of suffering. The Bhagavad Gita's emphasis on dharma, on fulfilling one's duty, resonated deeply with my desire to create positive change in the wake of tragedy. Chanakya's wisdom, with its focus on strategic action and ethical leadership, provided a practical guide for navigating the complexities of the legal system and advocating for broader reform. These philosophical frameworks weren't mere intellectual exercises; they were life rafts, providing solace and guidance amidst the turbulent waters of grief and anger.

The process of grieving, I discovered, is not a linear journey, but a cyclical one. There were days when the pain was overwhelming, when the memory of Connie's laughter felt like a phantom limb, a constant, aching reminder of what I had lost. There were moments when anger threatened to consume me once more, when the injustice of her passing seemed unbearable. But interspersed with these moments of intense sorrow were moments of quiet reflection, moments of peace, even joy. The memories of our life together, the shared laughter, the countless adventures, the intellectual sparring – these were not lost; they were woven into the fabric of my being, a testament to the enduring power of love.

The search for closure, then, is not about forgetting, but about integrating, about finding a way to live with the pain, to carry the memory of Connie with me, not as a burden, but as a source of strength and inspiration. It's about acknowledging the limitations of justice – the knowledge that no legal victory can ever truly replace the loss of a loved one – while still embracing the value of fighting for accountability and change. It's about recognizing the resilience of the human spirit, its capacity to heal, to adapt, to find meaning even in the face of unimaginable sorrow.

One of the unexpected blessings of this journey was the outpouring of support from friends, family, and even strangers who had been touched by Connie's life or who understood the depth of my pain. These connections, forged in the crucible of grief, became invaluable sources of comfort and strength. They reminded me that I was not alone in my struggle, that my pain was shared, understood, and validated. Their compassion and empathy provided a powerful antidote to the isolation that can often accompany profound loss.

The support extended beyond personal connections. The response to Connie's story, shared through various channels, revealed a widespread concern about the failures within the healthcare system. This collective outrage, this shared sense of injustice, transformed my personal grief into a call for broader systemic reform. It empowered me to channel my anger not into destructive self-pity, but into constructive action.

Writing this memoir itself has been a part of the healing process. The act of recounting our story, of reflecting on the complexities of our love and loss, has helped me to process my grief in a way that mere words could never capture. It has been an act of self-discovery, an exploration not only of Connie's life, but of my own, a journey of self-reflection prompted by the sudden and jarring disruption of her absence.

The quest for justice, the search for closure, the journey through grief – these are not separate endeavors, but intertwined threads woven into the tapestry of my life. They are intertwined with the profound love I shared with Connie, a love that transcends the boundaries of life and death, a love that continues to inspire me, to guide me, to sustain me. The pain remains, a constant companion, a poignant reminder of the preciousness of life and the devastating impact of loss. But interwoven with the pain is a profound gratitude for the time we shared, for the love we built, for the lessons learned, and for the enduring strength found in the face of unimaginable sorrow. The pursuit of justice became a means to honor Connie's memory, a path toward a more just and compassionate world. In doing so, I found a measure of peace, not through forgetting, but through remembrance, through action, and through a deepening understanding of the interconnectedness of life, love, and loss. It's a testament to the remarkable strength of the human spirit, capable of bearing the heaviest burdens and finding meaning even in the deepest darkness. The journey continues, evolving, transforming, and ever deepening. The love endures. The fight for justice continues. And the memory of Connie, my beautiful Connie, my two bodies and one soul, remains eternally vibrant. And that, I believe, is the truest form of closure.

# Krishnas Teachings on Acceptance

The searing pain of Connie's absence remained a constant companion, a phantom limb that ached with the memory of her touch, her laughter, the rhythm of our shared life. The initial shock had given way to a bone-deep weariness, a profound sense of displacement in a world that suddenly felt alien and empty. My crisis management training, usually my bedrock, offered little solace in this personal maelstrom. Logic and strategic planning couldn't mend a broken heart. What I needed was something more profound, a compass to guide me through the uncharted territory of grief. It was then that I turned, perhaps instinctively, to the wisdom I had gleaned over the years from spiritual and philosophical sources, specifically the teachings of Lord Krishna.

Krishna, the divine charioteer of the Bhagavad Gita, offered a pathway through the darkness, a perspective that transcended the immediacy of my sorrow. His teachings, embedded within the epic narrative of the Mahabharata, weren't about ignoring pain but about understanding its nature and finding a way to navigate it without being consumed by it. His message wasn't about passive resignation but about active acceptance, a conscious choice to engage with life's complexities, even amidst overwhelming sorrow.

The Gita's central theme, the battle between the Pandavas and the Kauravas, mirrors the internal struggle I faced. The war within me was between despair and the will to live, between the crushing weight of grief and the flicker of hope that refused to be extinguished. Krishna's counsel to Arjuna, hesitant to fight the seemingly invincible Kauravas, became my own guiding principle. Arjuna's doubt, his fear of the consequences of action, resonated deeply with my own feelings of paralysis and helplessness. Krishna's response, however, offered a potent antidote.

He urged Arjuna not to be paralyzed by fear, not to succumb to inaction, but to perform his duty, his *dharma*, without attachment to the outcome. This concept of *dharma*, often translated as righteous action or duty, is central to understanding Krishna's teachings on acceptance. It's not about accepting whatever happens passively but about engaging with life's challenges with a sense of purpose and responsibility, even when the path ahead is shrouded in uncertainty and pain. My *dharma*, I realized, was not only to grieve Connie's loss but also to seek justice for the negligence that hastened her passing, to honor her memory by striving for a fairer world.

Krishna emphasized the importance of *karma yoga*, the path of selfless action. By focusing on the act itself, rather than the fruits of the action, one transcends the anxieties and disappointments that inevitably accompany the pursuit of goals. In my grief, clinging to the hope of an impossible reversal of events was futile. The pursuit of justice, however, was a different matter. It was an act of honoring Connie's memory, a testament to our shared belief in fairness and accountability. It became my *karma yoga*, a way of channeling my pain into constructive action.

Furthermore, Krishna's teachings on *bhakti yoga*, the path of devotion, offered a profound source of comfort. While I grappled with my anger and frustration, the unwavering love I shared with Connie remained a constant source of strength. Remembering her, celebrating our life together, became a form of devotion, a way of keeping her spirit alive within me. It was a way of finding solace in the face of unimaginable loss, a way of acknowledging the preciousness of the life we had shared. This devotional aspect wasn't a religious act in a traditional sense; it was a deeply personal expression of love and remembrance, a spiritual practice that provided solace and strength.

The Bhagavad Gita also speaks to the ephemeral nature of life. Krishna reminds Arjuna, and by extension, me, that everything is in constant flux, that attachment to transient things inevitably leads to suffering. This didn't mean I should detach myself from Connie's memory, but it did mean I had to adjust my understanding of our relationship in the face of her death. Our bond, I realized, wasn't limited to the physical realm; it extended beyond death, into the realm of spirit. The love we shared, the memories we created, they transcended the physical separation.

This understanding helped to temper my anger and despair. The pursuit of justice became less about retribution and more about preventing similar tragedies from befalling others. It shifted the focus from the personal to the systemic, from the immediate pain to the long-term goal of improving healthcare practices and preventing medical negligence. This broader perspective, inspired by Krishna's wisdom, helped me to channel my grief into a constructive and meaningful pursuit.

Krishna's message of acceptance wasn't about passive resignation but about active engagement with life's challenges, about finding meaning and purpose even in the face of profound loss. It was about understanding the impermanence of all things, including life itself, and finding solace in the enduring power of love, in the shared memories that transcended the physical world.

While Krishna's teachings provided a spiritual framework for navigating my grief, the practical wisdom of Chanakya offered a complementary perspective, a grounding in the realities of the world. Chanakya, the ancient Indian strategist and statesman, emphasized the importance of *niti* , or righteous conduct, and *dharma* , in navigating life's complexities. His teachings, embodied in the Arthashastra, a treatise on statecraft and governance, provided a practical framework for understanding the systems and structures that shape our lives, including the healthcare system that failed Connie and me.

Chanakya's emphasis on justice, his understanding of the dynamics of power and influence, proved invaluable in my pursuit of accountability. His wisdom wasn't about blind faith or passive acceptance; it was about strategic action, about understanding the rules of the game and using them to achieve justice. The legal battles I faced were not simply emotional struggles but also strategic endeavors, requiring careful planning, meticulous evidence gathering, and unwavering determination. Chanakya's insights provided a practical lens through which to view these challenges, a framework for making sense of the complexities of the legal system.

His teachings on *artha* , or material prosperity, were also relevant. While not the primary focus of my journey, securing financial stability, and resolving the financial burden caused by Connie's illness and the subsequent legal battles, became a practical necessity. It was a matter of ensuring our financial security. Chanakya's focus on resource management and pragmatic decision-making guided me through the difficult financial and logistical tasks that followed her death.

The interplay between Krishna's spiritual guidance and Chanakya's pragmatic wisdom shaped my approach to grief, healing, and the pursuit of justice. It wasn't a matter of choosing one over the other, but of integrating both perspectives into a holistic approach to navigating my life after loss. Krishna's teachings provided the emotional and spiritual framework, while Chanakya's wisdom equipped me with the tools for practical action. This integration of spiritual understanding and rational action, of faith and reason, became the cornerstone of my journey through grief and towards a new understanding of life, love, and the pursuit of justice. The integration allowed me to reconcile my faith with my desire for accountability, and it allowed me to find meaning in my loss. It's a lesson that I believe is relevant for anyone navigating profound loss and seeking a path towards healing.

## Chanakyas Wisdom on Duty and Justice

The Bhagavad Gita, with its profound exploration of dharma and karma, had offered a framework for understanding Connie's passing within a larger cosmic context. It provided solace, a way to reconcile the unbearable pain with a sense of purpose, of continuing the dance of life even amidst profound loss. But Krishna's wisdom, however consoling, didn't provide a roadmap for navigating the labyrinthine corridors of the medical malpractice system. For that, I needed a different kind of guidance, a different lens through which to view the injustice I felt so keenly. That's where Chanakya's Arthashastra entered the picture.

Chanakya, the ancient Indian strategist and philosopher, wasn't concerned with cosmic harmonies or divine interventions. His focus was on the practicalities of governance, statecraft, and the pursuit of justice within the human realm. His Arthashastra, a treatise on political realism, offered a starkly different perspective from Krishna's spiritual idealism, yet, surprisingly, the two philosophies were not mutually exclusive. In fact, I found them to be complementary, two sides of the same coin – the coin of navigating life's complexities, particularly in moments of profound loss and injustice.

Chanakya's emphasis on *niti* (policy) and *nyaya* (justice) resonated deeply with my simmering anger and desire for accountability. His teachings on the importance of *dharma* (duty) provided a framework for action, a way to channel my grief into a purposeful pursuit of justice for Connie. While Krishna's teachings had helped me find acceptance in the face of loss, Chanakya's provided the tools to fight against the circumstances that contributed to it. The alleged negligence wasn't simply a personal tragedy; it was a failure of the system, a breach of the duty of care that every patient deserves. This wasn't just about my personal grief; it was about ensuring that others wouldn't suffer the same fate.

Chanakya's wisdom emphasized the importance of understanding the intricacies of power dynamics, the need for strategic thinking, and the crucial role of evidence in achieving justice. His emphasis on meticulous planning and execution mirrored my own crisis management training. I began to see my pursuit of justice not merely as an emotional response to grief, but as a strategic operation requiring careful planning, evidence gathering, and the skilled navigation of legal complexities. The methodical approach required, the gathering of medical records, the consultations with legal experts, the painstaking documentation – all of it resonated with Chanakya's practical approach to problem-solving.

The Arthashastra's emphasis on *danda* (punishment) initially struck me as harsh, perhaps even vengeful. But as I delved deeper, I realized Chanakya's concept of *danda* wasn't simply about retribution; it was about maintaining order, deterring future wrongdoing, and upholding justice. It was about ensuring that the system wasn't allowed to repeat its mistakes, that those responsible were held accountable for their actions, not simply for my personal satisfaction, but for the broader good. This shifted my perspective from a personal quest for vengeance to a commitment to broader systemic change. This broadened my focus from my specific grief to a desire for systemic reform within the medical community to prevent such tragedies from happening to others. This transformation was crucial in my healing journey.

The process of pursuing justice was grueling. It demanded patience, perseverance, and a deep well of emotional resilience. There were setbacks, moments of doubt, times when the sheer weight of the legal process threatened to overwhelm me. But Chanakya's teachings on perseverance, on the importance of staying the course even in the face of adversity, kept me going. His emphasis on meticulous planning, on anticipating obstacles and formulating contingency plans, proved invaluable in navigating the complexities of the legal system. Every consultation with my lawyers, every piece of evidence meticulously collected, every document reviewed – each act was a testament to Chanakya's pragmatic approach to achieving a desired outcome.

The legal battle itself was a harsh and often frustrating experience. The opposing side employed tactics designed to delay, obfuscate, and wear down our resolve. The sheer volume of paperwork, the seemingly endless depositions, the intricate legal maneuvers – it was a relentless assault on my time, my energy, and my emotional state. But I drew strength from Chanakya's teachings on resilience, on the importance of maintaining composure and strategic thinking even under pressure. His emphasis on understanding the motives and intentions of adversaries, on anticipating their moves and formulating effective countermeasures, became crucial in navigating the adversarial nature of the legal process.

Throughout this process, I learned to apply Chanakya's wisdom to the smaller challenges of daily life as well. The simple act of getting out of bed each morning, of maintaining a semblance of routine amidst the chaos of grief, required a level of discipline and intentionality that resonated with Chanakya's emphasis on self-control and mindful action. Every small victory, every milestone reached, fueled my determination and reinforced the value of his pragmatic approach to life's challenges.

The pursuit of justice wasn't just about winning a legal battle; it was about reclaiming a sense of control in a world that had felt utterly chaotic and unpredictable. It was about restoring a sense of purpose, a way to channel my grief into something meaningful and constructive. Chanakya's teachings provided not only a strategic framework but also a spiritual one, albeit a different kind from Krishna's. It was a spiritual path built not on divine grace but on human agency, on the power of reason, determination, and skillful action to create positive change in the world. It was about honoring Connie's memory not through passive mourning, but through active engagement with the world, through a commitment to justice and a dedication to ensuring that others wouldn't suffer the same fate.

In the end, the legal case was settled – a compromise, but one that provided a degree of closure and accountability. While the outcome didn't erase the pain, it brought a certain sense of justice, a validation of the ordeal Connie and I endured. The legal process, however, had taught me far more than just legal strategies. It had demonstrated the practical application of Chanakya's principles in real-life situations, a testament to the enduring relevance of his wisdom. The experience strengthened my conviction that the pursuit of justice, even amidst personal grief, is not only possible, but essential. It's a journey that requires both spiritual fortitude and strategic pragmatism, a blend of the wisdom of Lord Krishna and Chanakya. The two weren't opposing forces, but rather complementary aspects of a holistic approach to navigating life's most challenging moments. It's a testament to the power of integrating diverse perspectives in our pursuit of meaning and purpose, a journey that continues even after the loss of a loved one. And it's a journey that I believe resonates with anyone facing similar challenges. The lessons learned in this difficult period remain a valuable compass guiding me through life's subsequent journeys. The memories of Connie, the pain of her loss, the lessons learned through this protracted battle for justice – these continue to shape my life, constantly reminding me of the power of love, the importance of duty, and the enduring relevance of ancient wisdom in the modern world. The pursuit of justice, deeply intertwined with my grief, became a testament to the enduring power of love in the face of loss, a love that transcends even death.

# The Interplay of Faith and Reason

The settlement, while offering a measure of closure, didn't erase the chasm of grief that still yawned within me. The legal battle, fought with the strategic acumen Chanakya would have admired, had been a necessary act of justice, a way to acknowledge the wrong done to Connie and to find a path towards some semblance of peace. Yet, the peace remained elusive, a shimmering mirage in the desert of my sorrow. It was in this desolate landscape that I found myself grappling with the intricate interplay of faith and reason, two seemingly disparate forces that nevertheless intertwined deeply within my experience of loss.

My faith, nurtured over years of shared spiritual exploration with Connie, offered solace, a framework for understanding Connie's death not as a cruel, arbitrary end, but as a transition within a larger cosmic design. The Bhagavad Gita, with its emphasis on dharma and karma, provided a foundation for acceptance. Krishna's teachings resonated deeply, offering a perspective that transcended the immediate pain, reminding me that life, like a river, continues its flow, even amidst the most turbulent rapids. The concept of reincarnation, though intellectually challenging, provided a comfort, a whisper of hope that Connie's essence persisted, perhaps evolving in another form.

However, reason, too, played a vital role in processing my grief. The legal battles demanded a sharp, analytical mind, a rigorous application of logic and evidence. Chanakya's emphasis on pragmatism, on navigating the complexities of the human world with intelligence and strategic thinking, was invaluable. The pursuit of justice wasn't simply a matter of faith; it required meticulous planning, careful documentation, and a steadfast dedication to truth. Reason helped me to structure my emotions, channel my anger into constructive action, and maintain a sense of purpose amidst overwhelming despair.

The tension between these two forces, faith and reason, was not one of opposition, but of intricate symbiosis. They were two sides of the same coin, two lenses through which I viewed my reality. Faith offered a framework of meaning, a spiritual compass guiding me through the darkest hours. Reason provided the tools to navigate the practical challenges, to find a path towards healing and justice.

For instance, the initial shock of Connie's diagnosis and the subsequent progression of her illness spurred a frantic search for alternative treatments, fueled by a desperate hope, a faith that went beyond conventional medical approaches. Simultaneously, reason demanded that I remain grounded in reality, that I seek out reliable information, consult with multiple specialists, and make informed decisions based on evidence, not just wishful thinking. The battle against her illness was a relentless struggle between hope and acceptance, faith and pragmatism.

The legal process, even more so, highlighted the essential interplay of these two forces. My faith in the eventual triumph of justice, in the inherent rightness of seeking accountability, was a powerful motivator. Yet, the process itself demanded rigorous application of reason, a meticulous attention to detail, and an unflinching commitment to presenting a coherent and compelling case. The legal system, after all, operates on the basis of evidence, not solely on emotional pleas or spiritual beliefs.

During the protracted court hearings, I often found myself oscillating between these two realms. In moments of profound despair, I would turn to meditation, to the Bhagavad Gita for solace, finding strength in Krishna's unwavering message of dharma and the eternal nature of the soul. Yet, when facing the cold, hard facts of the courtroom, I relied on Chanakya's wisdom, organizing my thoughts, marshaling my evidence, and presenting a clear, logical case. It wasn't a matter of choosing between faith and reason; it was about integrating them, utilizing both for navigating the complexities of grief and the pursuit of justice.

Moreover, the conflict wasn't solely internal. It extended to the external world. The medical establishment, with its rigid hierarchies and often opaque decision-making processes, represented a challenge to my faith in the inherent goodness of human institutions. The experience shook my belief in the infallibility of medical expertise, exposing flaws and shortcomings that raised profound ethical questions. Yet, even amidst this disillusionment, reason propelled me forward, urging me to engage the system, to seek redress, not through blind faith in an idealized system, but through reasoned argument and the pursuit of evidence-based justice.

The experience taught me that grief is not a monolithic emotion, but a complex tapestry woven with threads of faith, reason, anger, acceptance, and ultimately, love. It's a journey fraught with challenges, requiring the navigation of both the spiritual and the secular realms. The integration of these seemingly disparate elements, faith and reason, became not only a coping mechanism but a source of strength, guiding me through the labyrinth of loss and towards a path of healing and acceptance. It became my own unique dharmic path.

The spiritual insights offered by Krishna provided a framework for understanding Connie's passing within a larger cosmic order, a sense of purpose that transcended the immediate pain. Chanakya's pragmatism offered a practical toolkit for navigating the intricacies of the legal system, seeking justice amidst intense emotional turmoil. It was the fusion of these two perspectives that proved invaluable in transforming my personal tragedy into a catalyst for growth, reflection, and ultimately, a path towards a renewed understanding of life's complexities.

This convergence wasn't merely an intellectual exercise; it was a lived experience, a testament to the power of integrating diverse perspectives in the face of profound loss. The process of navigating grief, intertwined with the pursuit of justice, required a sophisticated understanding of both spiritual and worldly realities. It was a process that demanded both emotional resilience and strategic intelligence, demanding that I draw upon the wisdom of ancient teachers – Krishna and Chanakya – to find my way through the darkness.

The journey, though painful, revealed the inherent strength within the human spirit, the capacity to find meaning and purpose even amidst the most devastating of circumstances. The blend of faith and reason proved not to be a dichotomy, but a powerful synergy, a testament to the human capacity to integrate seemingly disparate elements into a coherent and meaningful whole. This integration, this ability to draw upon both spiritual solace and pragmatic action, proved not only a survival mechanism but a springboard for growth and renewal. The lessons learned in this crucible of grief remain etched into my consciousness, shaping my outlook on life, loss, and the enduring power of love.

The pursuit of justice, far from being a mere legal battle, became a spiritual quest, a testament to Connie's memory, and a validation of our shared journey. It was a process of confronting the raw realities of human fallibility, the limitations of even the most sophisticated systems, and the enduring power of love to transcend even death. It was through this challenging process that I discovered the profound interplay of faith and reason, the integration of spiritual solace and pragmatic action, shaping my understanding of grief and life itself. The wisdom of both Krishna and Chanakya proved invaluable, illuminating the path through the darkest hours and guiding me toward a new dawn. And it is this journey, this profound and multifaceted experience of grief and its eventual transcendence, that forms the core of this narrative, a testament to the enduring power of love and the resilience of the human spirit. The lingering echoes of grief, however, continue to resonate, a constant reminder of Connie's presence, a bittersweet melody woven into the fabric of my life. This journey, while deeply personal, is also a testament to the universal human experience of loss, offering perhaps a small measure of comfort and understanding to those who have traveled, or are still traversing, this difficult path.

# Finding Meaning in Suffering

The legal battle concluded, the settlement funds deposited, yet the emptiness remained. The ache in my chest was not simply the physical absence of Connie's body beside mine; it was a hollowness that resonated in the very core of my being. The world, once vibrant with our shared laughter and dreams, had become muted, the colors drained from its palette. The justice I had sought, the accountability achieved, offered a fragile sense of closure, but it did little to mend the shattered fragments of my heart. It was in this profound desolation that I turned, almost instinctively, to the wisdom of ancient texts, seeking solace and meaning within their pages.

Lord Krishna, the divine charioteer in the Bhagavad Gita, speaks of dharma, of duty and righteousness. He urges Arjuna, paralyzed by grief and indecision, to act, to fulfill his responsibility despite the pain, to find his purpose in the face of seemingly insurmountable odds. His teachings resonated deeply, echoing within the chambers of my grief. My dharma, I realized, was not simply to mourn Connie's loss, but to honor her memory, to celebrate her life, and to continue living, not for myself alone, but in a way that would reflect the values we had shared, the love we had built together. This was not an easy path. The weight of sorrow pressed down upon me, a crushing burden that threatened to suffocate me. But Krishna's words, imbued with divine compassion and unwavering strength, offered a lifeline, a pathway through the darkness.

The Gita's lessons, however, were not merely passive comfort; they demanded active engagement. They spoke of karma, of action and consequence, of the interconnectedness of all things. My grief, I realized, was not simply a personal tragedy, but a part of a larger cosmic dance, a reflection of the cyclical nature of life and death. This understanding, though initially unsettling, gradually provided a framework for understanding, a way to contextualize my suffering within a broader perspective. It allowed me to move beyond the self-pity that threatened to consume me, and to embrace a more holistic view of existence.

Chanakya, the master strategist, offered a different kind of wisdom, a more pragmatic approach to navigating the complexities of life. His Arthashastra, a treatise on statecraft and governance, speaks of the importance of clear thinking, strategic planning, and decisive action. While seemingly far removed from the realm of personal grief, Chanakya's wisdom proved surprisingly relevant. The methodical approach I had employed in pursuing justice, the strategic planning involved in the legal battle, reflected the principles of the Arthashastra. In the face of overwhelming grief, the discipline of clear thinking and decisive action allowed me to focus on practical matters, to navigate the complexities of probate, insurance claims, and the myriad of practical issues that emerged in the aftermath of Connie's death. These tasks, while demanding and often emotionally taxing, provided a sense of control, a counterpoint to the pervasive feeling of helplessness.

The contrasting wisdom of Krishna and Chanakya, the spiritual and the pragmatic, became intertwined threads in the tapestry of my healing process. Krishna provided the spiritual framework, a lens through which I could understand my suffering within a larger context. Chanakya provided the practical tools, the strategies and tactics that enabled me to navigate the complexities of life, to manage the practical realities of grief and loss. The integration of these two seemingly disparate perspectives proved invaluable, offering me a holistic approach to coping with my loss.

The process was not linear. There were days when the darkness seemed insurmountable, when the weight of grief threatened to crush me. There were moments when anger flared, when the injustice of Connie's death felt unbearable. But the wisdom of Krishna and Chanakya, the lessons gleaned from their ancient texts, provided a compass, guiding me through the storms and toward a calmer sea. I found myself drawing parallels between the challenges they faced and my own, finding solace in their experiences, their struggles, and their eventual triumphs.

Krishna's journey, as depicted in the Bhagavad Gita, is one of self-discovery and the acceptance of one's dharma. Arjuna, overwhelmed by grief and doubt, learns to transcend his personal suffering through action, through the fulfillment of his duty. This mirrored my own experience. The pursuit of justice, the methodical process of securing accountability, became a form of action, a way of honoring Connie's memory, of fighting for her, even in her death. It was a way of asserting my own sense of purpose, of finding meaning amidst the chaos.

Chanakya's life, though less shrouded in mythology than Krishna's, is no less compelling. His strategic brilliance, his ability to navigate the treacherous currents of political intrigue, reflected a profound understanding of human nature, of power, and of the consequences of actions. His story, too, resonated deeply, offering a practical framework for navigating the complexities of my grief. The careful planning, the strategic approach I adopted in dealing with the legal and financial aftermath of Connie's death, reflected Chanakya's meticulous attention to detail and his unwavering commitment to achieving his goals. His unwavering focus on pragmatism, even in the face of emotional turmoil, allowed me to navigate the complex realities of the situation.

The wisdom of these two figures, though separated by centuries and vastly different contexts, found common ground in the importance of action, of purpose, and of the acceptance of life's impermanence. Krishna urged acceptance of one's dharma, the path that is set before each individual, regardless of the suffering. Chanakya's pragmatic approach provided the means to navigate the path, to overcome obstacles, and to find a way to move forward. Together, they illuminated a path for me through the darkest hours, guiding me towards a new understanding of life, death, and the enduring power of love.

The search for meaning in suffering is not a passive endeavor; it is an active, ongoing process. It is a journey of self-discovery, of grappling with the realities of loss, and of finding a new purpose in the face of overwhelming grief. It is a journey that requires both spiritual solace and pragmatic action, the wisdom of both Krishna and Chanakya, to guide the way. For me, this journey became a testament to the enduring power of love, a tribute to Connie's life, and a testament to the resilience of the human spirit. The grief, the pain, remains, a bittersweet melody that weaves through the fabric of my life. But through this process, I found a new rhythm, a new melody, one imbued with a deeper understanding of life's intricacies, and a renewed appreciation for the enduring power of love. This, ultimately, became my meaning, my purpose, my solace in the aftermath of loss. The journey continues, a testament to the interconnectedness of life, death, and the unwavering power of the human spirit to find meaning, even amidst the deepest sorrow. The legacy of love, forged in forty-one years of shared existence, remains, a beacon guiding me through the darkness, a testament to the enduring power of a love that transcends even death. The silence, once a deafening void, is now filled with the echoes of memories, whispers of laughter, and the enduring presence of Connie's spirit, a constant reminder of the life we shared, and a guiding force on the path ahead. The pain remains, but it is tempered by the knowledge that love endures, a constant, immutable force in the universe, a force that continues to shape my life, even in the absence of the one I loved. This understanding, hard-won through the crucible of grief, is my solace, my meaning, my dharma.

# Integrating Spiritual Wisdom into Daily Life

The legal battles concluded, the settlement secured, yet the chasm within remained. The quiet of my house, once filled with Connie's laughter and the gentle clinking of teacups, now echoed with a silence that felt both oppressive and isolating. The search for justice had been a necessary act, a furious striving against the injustice of Connie's untimely passing. It provided a semblance of closure, a sense of having fought for her, even in death. Yet, the void persisted, a constant, gnawing reminder of her absence. It was in this desolate landscape that I sought refuge in the familiar comfort of spiritual and philosophical wisdom. It wasn't a sudden, dramatic shift, but a gradual immersion, a slow and deliberate process of integrating ancient teachings into the fabric of my daily life.

My grief was a tempest, a relentless storm raging within me. The rational part of my mind, honed by years spent in crisis management, urged me toward order, toward structure. But the emotional maelstrom threatened to overwhelm, to drown me in its relentless waves. It was in this chaotic sea that I found anchors in the teachings of Lord Krishna and Chanakya – seemingly disparate figures, yet both offering profound insights into navigating life's complexities, particularly in the face of profound loss. Krishna, the divine charioteer, guided me towards understanding the impermanence of the material world, the cyclical nature of life and death, the importance of detached action, and the path to inner peace. Chanakya, the master strategist, provided a framework for navigating the practical aspects of life, emphasizing the importance of clear thinking, careful planning, and the essential need to maintain a sense of purpose, even amidst overwhelming sorrow.

Krishna's Bhagavad Gita, a text I had encountered many times throughout my life, now resonated with a new and profound urgency. His words, once abstract philosophical concepts, became visceral truths, reflecting the realities of my own suffering. The concept of *karma yoga* – selfless action without attachment to results – became my guiding principle. The legal battle, however painful, had been a form of karma yoga. I had acted, not out of a desire for revenge, but out of a sense of duty, a commitment to ensuring accountability for Connie's suffering. Now, the process of healing also became an act of karma yoga. Each day, I consciously sought to engage in activities that would bring some degree of peace and purpose, even as my heart ached with an unbearable longing.

This wasn't about forcing myself to be happy; it was about accepting the reality of my grief while simultaneously engaging in activities that nurtured my spirit and honored Connie's memory. I resumed my painting, finding solace in the creative process, translating my grief and memories onto the canvas. The colors, once muted and somber, slowly began to regain vibrancy, mirroring the subtle shifts in my own emotional landscape. Each brushstroke was a prayer, a meditation, a way to channel my sorrow into something beautiful and enduring.

The Gita's emphasis on *dharma* – fulfilling one's duty – became central to my daily life. My dharma was no longer solely defined by professional accomplishments. It now encompassed the grieving process itself, the dedication to healing, and the commitment to preserving Connie's legacy. I meticulously organized her papers, her artwork, her collection of cherished books. Each item held a memory, a fragment of our shared life, a testament to a love that transcended the boundaries of time and space. This was an act of reverence, a way of honoring her life, and, in a strange way, a way of keeping her close. It was a form of active remembering, a counterpoint to the numbness and despair.

Chanakya's teachings, far from being contradictory to Krishna's wisdom, provided a practical framework for integrating spiritual principles into my daily routine. Chanakya emphasized the importance of discipline, planning, and strategic thinking. These weren't qualities that would magically erase my grief, but they provided a much-needed sense of structure and control amidst the chaos. I established a daily routine, incorporating regular meditation, yoga, and walks in nature. These activities, while seemingly simple, provided a much-needed sense of grounding and helped regulate the emotional roller coaster of grief. The rhythmic nature of these practices became a balm, a way of soothing the agitated waters within.

The initial days were marked by a profound sense of disorientation. Even simple tasks felt overwhelming. But slowly, incrementally, I began to regain a sense of purpose. The disciplined application of Chanakya's principles helped me establish a routine, a framework for navigating my days. This structure wasn't meant to suppress my emotions; rather, it provided a container for them, a safe space within which I could process my grief without feeling completely overwhelmed.

I also began to explore other spiritual traditions, drawing inspiration from different philosophical perspectives. I reread the works of Rumi, finding comfort in his lyrical exploration of love, loss, and the divine. The Stoic philosophers, with their emphasis on inner resilience and acceptance, provided a framework for navigating the inevitable challenges of life. Each tradition offered a unique lens through which to examine my grief, providing new insights and helping me to broaden my understanding of life's complexities.

The process wasn't always easy. There were days when the pain was overwhelming, when the weight of my sorrow threatened to crush me. But through it all, the principles of Krishna and Chanakya served as guiding lights, providing a framework for navigating the darkness and finding meaning amidst the despair. The integration of these spiritual and philosophical insights wasn't a passive act; it was an active, conscious endeavor, a constant process of learning, adapting, and growing.

The act of writing this memoir itself became a form of spiritual practice. It was a way of processing my grief, of giving voice to my sorrow, of sharing my journey with others. Each word written was a step forward, a testament to the enduring power of love, a celebration of Connie's life, and a testament to the resilience of the human spirit. Through the process, I found a new understanding of my own strength and capacity for healing. The pain persists, but it's now intertwined with a sense of purpose, a recognition of the enduring power of love, and a profound appreciation for the fragility and beauty of life.

The journey continues. The silence is no longer a void, but a space filled with memories, with the echoes of laughter, and the enduring presence of Connie's spirit. The grief, like a persistent melody, weaves through the fabric of my days, but it's tempered by a newfound understanding, a deeper appreciation for the interconnectedness of life, death, and the unwavering strength of the human spirit. My dharma, my duty, is now to honor her memory, to continue to live a life filled with purpose, and to share the lessons I have learned with others who are navigating their own paths through the darkness. The journey is long, but the path is lit by the enduring flame of love, a flame that burns brightly even amidst the shadows of grief. The search for meaning continues, a testament to the enduring power of the human spirit to find solace, even in the deepest sorrow. And in the quiet moments, when the pain subsides, I find myself enveloped in the warm embrace of love – a love that transcends the boundaries of life and death, a love that continues to shape my world, even in Connie's absence. It is in this enduring love, this enduring connection, that I find true peace, a peace that is both profound and profoundly personal. It is the essence of "Two Bodies & One Soul".

insights and helping me to broaden my understanding of life's complexities.

The process wasn't always easy. There were days when the pain was overwhelming, when the weight of my sorrow threatened to crush me. But through it all, the principles of Krishna and Chanakya served as guiding lights, providing a framework for navigating the darkness and finding meaning amidst the despair. The integration of these spiritual and philosophical insights wasn't a passive act; it was an active, conscious endeavor, a constant process of learning, adapting, and growing.

The act of writing this memoir itself became a form of spiritual practice. It was a way of processing my grief, of giving voice to my sorrow, of sharing my journey with others. Each word written was a step forward, a testament to the enduring power of love, a celebration of Connie's life, and a testament to the resilience of the human spirit. Through the process, I found a new understanding of my own strength and capacity for healing. The pain persists, but it's now intertwined with a sense of purpose, a recognition of the enduring power of love, and a profound appreciation for the fragility and beauty of life.

The journey continues. The silence is no longer a void, but a space filled with memories, with the echoes of laughter, and the enduring presence of Connie's spirit. The grief, like a persistent melody, weaves through the fabric of my days, but it's tempered by a newfound understanding, a deeper appreciation for the interconnectedness of life, death, and the unwavering strength of the human spirit. My dharma, my duty, is now to honor her memory, to continue to live a life filled with purpose, and to share the lessons I have learned with others who are navigating their own paths through the darkness. The journey is long, but the path is lit by the enduring flame of love, a flame that burns brightly even amidst the shadows of grief. The search for meaning continues, a testament to the enduring power of the human spirit to find solace, even in the deepest sorrow. And in the quiet moments, when the pain subsides, I find myself enveloped in the warm embrace of love – a love that transcends the boundaries of life and death, a love that continues to shape my world, even in Connie's absence. It is in this enduring love, this enduring connection, that I find true peace, a peace that is both profound and profoundly personal. It is the essence of "Two Bodies & One Soul".

# The Long Road to Healing

The initial months were a blur, a relentless tide of grief threatening to pull me under. Each sunrise felt like a betrayal, a stark reminder of a world irrevocably altered. Connie's absence was a physical ache, a void that echoed in every corner of our home, in the quiet spaces between breaths. The routines we had shared – the morning coffee, the evening walks, the quiet companionship over a book – were now shards of memory, cutting into the fabric of my present. Sleep offered no respite, only a tormented cycle of dreams and nightmares, punctuated by the sudden jolt of waking, the crushing realization that she was truly gone.

My days were consumed by a suffocating sadness, a profound loneliness that transcended the mere absence of her physical presence. It was a loneliness of the soul, a deep yearning for the shared intimacy, the unspoken understanding that had defined our forty-one years together. Even the simplest tasks – preparing a meal, choosing an outfit, watching a sunset – were fraught with a poignant reminder of her absence. The vibrant tapestry of our life together had been ripped apart, leaving behind a tattered and frayed remnant.

My background in crisis management, ironically, offered little solace in this personal crisis. The tools I had used to navigate professional turmoil felt utterly inadequate in the face of such devastating personal loss. The structured approaches, the logical frameworks, the meticulous planning – all seemed irrelevant, almost offensive, when confronted with the chaotic landscape of my grief. The strategies that had served me well in the boardroom felt weak and fragile in the face of such profound and raw emotion.

Yet, even in the depths of my despair, a tiny ember of resilience began to flicker. It was a faint spark, barely noticeable against the overwhelming darkness, but it was there, nonetheless. It fueled a quiet determination to navigate this uncharted territory, to find a path toward healing, however long and arduous it might be. It was a recognition that while my world had been irrevocably changed, my life was not over. There was still a future to be found, a path to be carved amidst the wreckage of my loss.

The initial steps were hesitant, almost imperceptible. Simple acts of self-care – taking a walk, preparing a healthy meal, spending a few minutes in quiet contemplation – became acts of defiance against the crushing weight of my grief. Each completed task, no matter how insignificant, represented a small victory, a testament to my enduring spirit. I began to re-engage with the things that once brought me joy, though the experience was often bittersweet, tinged with a profound sense of melancholy. Revisiting our favorite haunts, reading books that we had shared, listening to the music we had both loved – these became rituals of remembrance, a way of keeping her memory alive.

The support of friends and family proved invaluable during this difficult period. Their presence, their words of comfort, their unwavering support, created a lifeline, a source of strength that pulled me through the darkest of times. The kindness of strangers, the unexpected gestures of compassion, also offered unexpected comfort. These acts of human connection, however small, served as a reminder that I was not alone in my sorrow, that there was still a world beyond my grief.

Slowly, painstakingly, I began to rebuild my life. I returned to work, finding a strange comfort in the structure and routine of my professional life. The demands of my career, while initially overwhelming, provided a much-needed distraction from the intensity of my grief. It gave me a sense of purpose, a feeling of accomplishment, something concrete to focus on amidst the swirling emotions.

But the healing process was not linear. There were days when the grief would return with a vengeance, engulfing me in a wave of sorrow that threatened to overwhelm me. There were moments when the pain felt unbearable, when the weight of my loss seemed too heavy to bear. Yet, through these difficult moments, I learned to navigate the complexities of grief, to accept its presence without allowing it to consume me entirely. I came to understand that healing is not about erasing the pain but learning to live with it, to integrate it into the tapestry of my life.

The pursuit of justice became an unexpected source of strength and purpose. The legal battle against the medical negligence I believed contributed to Connie's death was arduous and emotionally draining. Yet, the fight itself became a way of channeling my anger and frustration, transforming them into a driving force to fight for accountability, to prevent other families from suffering similar tragedies. The process, while fraught with challenges, gave me a sense of agency, a feeling of control in a world that had felt utterly beyond my grasp.

My spiritual and philosophical reflections also played a significant role in my healing journey. The teachings of Lord Krishna and Chanakya, which had offered solace during Connie's illness, continued to provide guidance and wisdom. Their words of acceptance, surrender, and the importance of duty resonated deeply with my experiences. The concept of dharma, the righteous path, became a compass, guiding my actions and decisions. Through meditation, prayer, and contemplation, I found a profound sense of peace and acceptance.

The process of rebuilding involved not just my external circumstances but also a profound re-evaluation of my identity and purpose. Losing Connie forced me to confront fundamental questions about who I was, what mattered most, and what I wanted to achieve in the remaining years of my life. The answer was simple, but profound: I wanted to honor Connie's memory, to live a life worthy of the love we shared. This meant continuing to pursue justice, to fight for better healthcare, to dedicate myself to causes that were meaningful to both of us.

Re-establishing connections with friends and family became essential in my healing journey. The support and understanding I received were instrumental in helping me navigate my grief. The reconnection reminded me that I was not alone, that there was a network of people who cared and who would accompany me on this difficult path. The sharing of stories, memories, and support created a powerful sense of community and helped me to feel less isolated in my sorrow.

Learning to embrace new beginnings was a challenging but rewarding process. It meant stepping outside of my comfort zone, taking risks, and exploring new avenues. It meant opening myself to the possibility of finding joy and purpose again. It was a recognition that life continues even after profound loss, that there is space for new experiences, new relationships, and new opportunities for happiness. The healing process was not about replacing Connie but about creating space in my life for new chapters, new experiences, and new joys. The path forward was not about forgetting but about remembering, cherishing the past, while embracing the possibilities of the future. The healing journey is a marathon, not a sprint, requiring patience, perseverance, and a commitment to self-care. It's about integrating the pain, finding meaning, and celebrating the enduring power of love.

# Redefining Identity and Purpose

The initial shock had begun to subside, replaced by a gnawing emptiness. It wasn't just the physical absence of Connie; it was the absence of our shared identity. For forty-one years, our lives had been inextricably interwoven. We were "two bodies and one soul," as I'd often described us, a single entity expressed in two forms. Now, that entity felt fractured, leaving me adrift in a sea of unfamiliar solitude. Who was I, without her?

The question echoed in the silence of our home, a silence that had become both oppressive and strangely liberating. The silence was a canvas, blank yet brimming with potential. Before, our lives had been a vibrant tapestry woven with shared dreams, ambitions, and routines. Now, the threads were severed, leaving me to decide how to reweave them, or perhaps, to create an entirely new pattern.

My professional life, typically a source of focus and accomplishment, offered little solace. My work in crisis management, ironically, had prepared me for many things, but nothing could have prepared me for the sheer intensity of this personal crisis. My expertise in navigating complex situations, in analyzing data and formulating strategies, felt utterly inadequate in the face of my grief. The rational, analytical mind that had served me so well in countless professional challenges seemed to falter, overwhelmed by the emotional maelstrom that consumed me. I found myself retreating from my colleagues, my work becoming a mere distraction, a hollow echo of my former engagement. The crisp lines of my spreadsheets no longer offered clarity; they merely underscored the gaping void in my life.

Yet, within this void, a glimmer of something else began to emerge. A new sense of introspection, a deeper understanding of my own capabilities and limitations. The loss of Connie had forced me to confront aspects of myself that had been overshadowed by our shared existence. It was a painful process, akin to excavating a long-buried foundation, but the unearthed fragments, however fractured, held the potential for a new structure.

My spiritual practices, previously a background hum in my life, now became a lifeline. The wisdom of Lord Krishna and Chanakya, figures I'd long admired, offered unexpected comfort. Krishna's teachings on dharma, on the importance of fulfilling one's duty, resonated deeply. My duty, I realized, was not merely to mourn Connie, but to honor her memory by living a life that reflected her values and the love we had shared. Chanakya's pragmatism, his focus on action and strategic thinking, provided a framework for navigating the practical challenges that lay ahead. His emphasis on justice became a driving force in my quest to understand and challenge the perceived medical negligence that had, in my view, contributed to Connie's suffering and death.

The fight for justice became a surprisingly powerful catalyst for rebuilding my life. The meticulous research, the relentless pursuit of accountability, gave my days a structure, a focus that grief had initially eroded. It was a way to channel my anger and despair into productive action. Each legal victory, each acknowledgment of wrongdoing, felt like a small step towards healing. The pursuit of justice, I discovered, wasn't merely about seeking retribution; it was about reclaiming agency, about reasserting my control in a world that had felt utterly out of control.

Beyond the legal battle, my search for purpose extended to other areas. Connie and I had shared a passion for travel, for immersing ourselves in different cultures and landscapes. I found solace in returning to these shared passions, but this time, alone. The journeys were different, naturally, tinged with bittersweet memories, but they were also opportunities for self-discovery. The solitude forced me to confront my own thoughts and feelings, to appreciate the world around me in a new light. Each sunrise, once a painful reminder of Connie's absence, now held the potential for fresh perspectives, new experiences, and newfound appreciation for the beauty and resilience of life.

Another significant aspect of this redefinition involved confronting my own mortality. Connie's death had brought my own finitude into sharp focus. The fear of death, which I had previously suppressed, now became a catalyst for profound self-reflection. I began to question my priorities, the values that guided my life. I revisited my goals, shedding those that no longer resonated with my newly defined sense of self, and embracing new aspirations rooted in a deeper understanding of my own limitations and potential.

This process wasn't linear; it was messy, unpredictable, and often agonizing. There were days when the grief overwhelmed me, when the emptiness seemed insurmountable. But through the process, I discovered an inner strength I never knew I possessed. I learned to embrace the vulnerability of grief, to allow myself to feel the pain without allowing it to consume me entirely. I learned to cultivate self-compassion, recognizing that my journey was unique and that there was no right or wrong way to grieve.

Redefining my identity wasn't about replacing Connie; it was about creating space for a new chapter in my life, a chapter informed by the lessons learned during our time together. It was about honoring her memory by living a life that was both meaningful and fulfilling, even amidst profound loss. It was about discovering new ways to express my love for her, to keep her spirit alive within me. The love we had shared, the "two bodies and one soul," remained a constant, a powerful source of strength and inspiration in my journey towards rebuilding and rediscovering myself.

The challenge wasn't simply to survive but to thrive, to find purpose and meaning in the face of devastating loss. My journey wasn't a return to a previous self, but a transformation, a metamorphosis fueled by grief, tempered by wisdom, and guided by a deep-seated commitment to honoring the enduring legacy of my love for Connie. The new identity I was forging was not a replacement for the life we shared, but rather a testament to its enduring impact on my life and my soul. It was a recognition that even in the depths of grief, the human spirit possesses an incredible capacity for resilience, for growth, and for finding new paths towards meaning and fulfillment.

This new chapter wasn't about forgetting; it was about remembering, celebrating the past, while embracing the possibilities of the future. It was about integrating the pain, finding meaning in loss, and celebrating the enduring power of love, a love that transcended even the finality of death. The process was, and continues to be, a journey of constant rediscovery, a testament to the enduring power of the human spirit to navigate even the most profound losses and emerge stronger, wiser, and more deeply connected to the essence of what it means to truly live. The path forward was not a straight line, but a winding road filled with unexpected turns, unexpected joys, and a profound understanding of the enduring strength of the human heart. It was, and remains, a journey of healing, of resilience, and of rediscovery. A testament to the unyielding power of love, even in the face of unimaginable loss. The pain may linger, but so does the love, a love that continues to shape and define who I am, who I have become. A love that transcends even death itself.

## The Importance of SelfCare

The initial shock of Connie's absence had given way to a persistent ache, a hollow space where our intertwined lives once resided. The silence in the house was deafening, a stark contrast to the vibrant symphony of our shared existence. Yet, within the depths of this grief, a nascent understanding began to dawn: my journey through this unimaginable loss required more than just mourning; it demanded a conscious commitment to self-care. This wasn't about selfishness; it was about survival. It was about recognizing that I couldn't pour from an empty cup. To honor Connie's memory and to continue living a life worthy of the love we shared, I needed to replenish myself, to nurture my physical and emotional well-being.

This realization didn't come easily. The initial months were a blur of numbness, punctuated by waves of crippling sorrow. Sleep became a battlefield, each night a harrowing struggle against the relentless tide of memories. Food held little appeal; meals were often skipped, replaced by a gnawing emptiness that mirrored the void in my heart. Physical activity, once a cherished part of our lives – our long walks, our weekend hikes – seemed an insurmountable task. My body mirrored my soul: depleted, fragile, and aching.

The turning point came unexpectedly, during a visit from my nephew, Rohan. He watched me with a quiet concern that pierced my self-imposed isolation. "Uncle Pradeep," he said gently, "you need to take care of yourself. Connie wouldn't want you to let this consume you." His words, simple yet profound, struck a chord. Connie, always practical and pragmatic, had always emphasized the importance of self-preservation, even in the face of adversity. Her voice, though silent, resonated in my heart. It was a stark reminder that my grief, while profound and justifiable, shouldn't become a license for self-neglect.

The path to self-care wasn't linear; it was a winding road paved with small, incremental steps. First, I started with the basics: ensuring I ate regular meals, even if it was just a simple bowl of soup. I forced myself to drink plenty of water, combating the dehydration that had crept in unnoticed. I began with short walks in the park near our home, initially struggling with each step, the weight of my sorrow pressing down on me. Gradually, these walks became longer, more purposeful. The rhythmic movement, the fresh air, the quiet beauty of nature – it all served as a gentle balm to my wounded spirit.

Sleep remained elusive for a long time. But I started practicing mindfulness techniques, learning to quiet the relentless chatter in my mind. I began reading again, immersing myself in books that offered solace and perspective – philosophical treatises, spiritual texts, biographies of individuals who had navigated their own profound losses. These weren't distractions; they were pathways to understanding, to finding meaning in the chaos.

I discovered the power of small rituals, practices that provided a sense of normalcy and routine amidst the turbulence. I started preparing simple meals, a stark contrast to our once elaborate culinary adventures. Yet, the act of cooking, of nurturing myself through food, became a form of self-love, a way of honoring Connie's memory by attending to the basic needs she would have insisted upon. I started tending to our garden, weeding, watering, nurturing the plants she had so lovingly cared for. The act of nurturing life, however small, became a form of self-healing.

I sought professional help, recognizing the limitations of my own coping mechanisms. Therapy wasn't a sign of weakness; it was a courageous act of self-preservation. My therapist, a wise and compassionate woman, helped me navigate the labyrinth of my grief, providing a safe space to explore my emotions without judgment. She helped me understand the stages of grief, reassuring me that my experiences were normal, that the pain wouldn't last forever.

Beyond the physical and emotional, self-care extended to my spiritual well-being. I renewed my practice of meditation, finding solace in the quiet moments of introspection. I revisited spiritual texts, drawing strength and wisdom from ancient teachings. The Bhagavad Gita, with its timeless wisdom on dharma and the acceptance of life's impermanence, became a constant companion. Chanakya's teachings on resilience and strategic action provided a framework for navigating the challenges ahead. These were not mere escapist fantasies; they were tools, guiding principles that helped me find meaning and direction amidst the uncertainty.

The pursuit of justice, fueled by my anger and frustration over Connie's untimely death, also became a form of self-care. It was an act of channeling my grief into productive action, preventing it from consuming me entirely. The legal battle was arduous, demanding, and emotionally draining. Yet, the process of seeking accountability, of ensuring that others wouldn't suffer a similar fate due to medical negligence, gave my grief a purpose, a focus beyond the immediate pain. It was a way of transforming anger into action, a powerful cathartic experience that helped to alleviate some of my burden.

My self-care journey was not without its setbacks. There were days when the grief overwhelmed me, when the pain seemed insurmountable. There were times when I relapsed into old habits, neglecting my physical and emotional well-being. But each time, I reminded myself of Connie's presence, of her unwavering support, of her belief in my strength. These memories, once a source of unbearable pain, became a source of strength, a guiding light in my darkest moments.

The journey of rebuilding and rediscovering myself after Connie's death has been a testament to the resilience of the human spirit. Self-care, in all its multifaceted forms, has been instrumental in this process. It has been a journey of learning, of adapting, of discovering new strengths and coping mechanisms. It has been a path toward acceptance, not forgetting Connie, but learning to live with her absence, to find joy again, to honor her memory by embracing life's possibilities. It is an ongoing process, a continuous commitment to nurturing my physical, emotional, and spiritual well-being – a testament to the enduring power of love, a love that continues to shape and define who I am, even in the face of profound loss. It is a journey of healing, of rediscovery, and of celebrating the enduring flame of a love that transcends even death itself. And that, I believe, is a worthy tribute to Connie, to our forty-one years together, to the unique bond we shared – two bodies, one soul.

# Reestablishing Connections

The initial shock of Connie's passing had eventually subsided, replaced by a persistent, gnawing ache. The silence in our home, once filled with laughter, music, and the murmur of conversation, now echoed with an emptiness that seemed to swallow me whole. Yet, amidst the profound grief, a quiet understanding began to emerge: my survival, my ability to navigate this unimaginable loss, depended not just on mourning, but on actively rebuilding my life. It wasn't a selfish act; it was an act of self-preservation, a recognition that I couldn't pour from an empty cup and still expect to nurture anything, let alone myself. To honor Connie's memory, to live a life worthy of the love we shared, I needed to refill myself, to tend to my physical and emotional well-being. This realization marked a turning point, a shift from passive acceptance of grief to active engagement in the process of healing.

One of the most crucial aspects of this rebuilding process was the re-establishment of connections. The outpouring of support in the immediate aftermath of Connie's death had been overwhelming, a comforting wave of love and compassion from family, friends, and even acquaintances. But as the initial flurry of condolences subsided, the silence returned, amplifying the void. I realized then that the support I needed wasn't just about receiving sympathy; it was about actively cultivating meaningful relationships, about reconnecting with the people who had sustained me throughout my life, and about forging new connections that would provide solace and strength in the years to come.

My relationship with my children took on a new dimension. Before Connie's illness, our family dynamics had been comfortable, almost predictable. We had a routine, a rhythm to our lives, and while we cherished our time together, there was an underlying assumption of permanence. Connie's passing shattered that assumption, exposing a vulnerability that forced us to confront our emotions, to openly share our grief, and to find strength in our shared bond. We began having longer conversations, sharing memories of Connie, not only remembering the joyous moments, but also the challenges and conflicts, acknowledging the imperfections that made our family unit uniquely ours. These conversations were not easy; they were often painful, bringing tears and intense emotions to the surface. But through them, we forged a stronger, more compassionate connection, a bond built on shared loss and mutual support. We learned to lean on each other, offering each other comfort and understanding during our individual struggles. Our family dinners, previously a matter of routine, became sacred spaces, where we honored Connie's memory by sharing stories and maintaining the traditions she had cherished.

My friendships also underwent a transformation. Some relationships, tested by the crucible of grief, emerged stronger than ever before. Others faded, revealing unspoken tensions or incompatible coping mechanisms. I learned to distinguish between those who genuinely offered support and those whose presence felt more like an obligation. I discovered the value of authentic connection, of sharing my vulnerability without fear of judgment. With some friends, our conversations revolved around memories of Connie, sharing anecdotes and celebrating her life. With others, the focus shifted to mutual support, sharing our individual struggles and finding solace in our shared humanity. This process of rediscovering and nurturing friendships wasn't always easy. It required a level of vulnerability that I hadn't previously embraced. I had to overcome the reluctance to burden others with my grief, the ingrained tendency to suppress my emotions and maintain a facade of strength. But gradually, I learned to accept support, to acknowledge my need for companionship and understanding.

Beyond my existing relationships, I also made a conscious effort to cultivate new connections. I joined a support group for widowed men, a space where I could share my experiences with others who understood the unique challenges of grief. The group offered a sense of community, a shared experience that transcended the individual pain. I found solace in listening to others' stories, realizing that my grief wasn't unique, that others had navigated similar emotional landscapes. This helped to alleviate the feeling of isolation that often accompanies profound loss. The group also provided practical advice and coping strategies, reminding me that I wasn't alone in my journey.

My connection with my spiritual community deepened as well. The solace I found in meditation and prayer became even more crucial. Connie and I had always shared a deep appreciation for spiritual practices, and her absence only intensified my need for connection with something larger than myself. The regular practice of mindfulness helped me to regulate my emotions, to find moments of peace amidst the chaos of grief. I found comfort in the wisdom of ancient teachings, finding resonance with the teachings of Lord Krishna on acceptance and detachment, and the pragmatic insights of Chanakya on navigating life's challenges. These philosophical perspectives provided a framework for understanding my grief, for finding meaning in suffering, and for accepting the impermanence of life.

Re-establishing connections extended beyond personal relationships. I reconnected with my passion for writing, pouring my grief, my anger, and my love for Connie into this memoir. The act of writing became a form of therapy, a way of processing my emotions and making sense of my loss. It was a way to honor Connie's memory, to share our story, and to leave a legacy of love and resilience. This process also inadvertently connected me with a wider audience, allowing me to engage in conversations with readers who had experienced similar losses, and to offer comfort and support through the sharing of my story.

The process of re-establishing connections wasn't simply about rebuilding my social network; it was about fostering a sense of belonging, of finding my place in the world after Connie's death. It involved being vulnerable, accepting support, and actively engaging in the healing process. It was about recognizing the importance of human connection, the profound impact of shared experiences, and the sustaining power of love and compassion. It wasn't about replacing Connie, but about enriching my life, finding new sources of joy, and honoring her memory by living fully and embracing the opportunities that life still held. The journey is ongoing, a testament to the resilience of the human spirit and the enduring power of love. It's a reminder that even in the darkest of times, the light of human connection can illuminate the path toward healing and rediscovery. The connections I've forged, both old and new, have become the pillars supporting me as I navigate this new chapter of my life. They are a constant reminder of Connie's legacy, and a source of strength in my continuing journey toward healing and self-discovery.

The legal battle surrounding Connie's illness and subsequent death, fueled by my anger and sense of injustice, became another unexpected avenue for connection. The process of pursuing justice, while emotionally draining, brought me into contact with lawyers, medical professionals, and other individuals involved in the legal system. These interactions, though often challenging, provided unexpected connections.

The shared pursuit of accountability fostered a sense of purpose, helping to channel my grief and anger into a constructive outlet. It's a complicated aspect of my journey, one that continues to unfold, but it has demonstrated the unexpected connections that can arise even from the most difficult of circumstances. The sense of justice is a powerful motivator, and the pursuit of it, while painful, has also brought about unforeseen connections and a renewed sense of purpose.

Moreover, reconnecting with my community in a broader sense helped redefine my role in the world. Volunteering at a local hospice, an organization that provided compassionate care similar to what Connie had received, became a powerful way to channel my grief into positive action. It wasn't about escaping my sorrow, but about transforming it into something meaningful. Connecting with other volunteers, sharing our common purpose, brought a sense of camaraderie and purpose. It was a way of giving back, a way of honoring Connie's memory by helping others navigate their own difficult journeys. The act of supporting others in their time of need was surprisingly healing. The empathetic connections I forged while volunteering helped alleviate my own sense of isolation and provided a powerful sense of purpose. It was a testament to the fact that even in the deepest sorrow, there's an opportunity to make a difference, to find meaning and connection beyond personal loss.

The healing process, therefore, isn't a linear progression; it's a continuous journey of growth and adaptation. It's a testament to the resilience of the human spirit, the capacity for love to endure even in the face of profound loss, and the transformative power of human connection. The re-establishment of connections—with family, friends, community, and even with myself—has been instrumental in my journey of rebuilding and rediscovering self. It's a process that continues to evolve, but it's a process that affirms the enduring truth that we are, ultimately, social creatures, and our connections to others are essential to our well-being. Through this process, I've learned that healing isn't just about overcoming grief, but about transforming it, finding strength in vulnerability, and celebrating the enduring power of love and human connection. The journey continues, but it's a journey I'm navigating with newfound purpose, resilience, and a deep appreciation for the connections that sustain me.

## Embracing New Beginnings

The initial shock had given way to a dull, persistent ache, a constant reminder of the void Connie had left behind. The quiet of our home, once filled with the symphony of our shared life, now felt oppressive, a suffocating silence that threatened to consume me. Yet, within that darkness, a flicker of understanding ignited. My survival, my ability to navigate this unimaginable loss, wasn't solely about mourning; it was about actively rebuilding my life. This wasn't selfishness; it was self-preservation. To honor Connie's memory, to live a life worthy of the love we shared, I needed to replenish myself, to tend to my physical and emotional well-being. This marked a pivotal shift, a transition from passive grieving to active engagement in healing.

This wasn't a simple, linear progression, but a continuous journey of growth and adaptation, a testament to the resilience of the human spirit. The capacity for love to endure, even in the face of profound loss, became increasingly apparent. The transformative power of human connection, too, became a cornerstone of my healing. Re-establishing connections—with family, friends, community, and even with myself—proved instrumental. It was a process that continues to evolve, but one that reaffirmed the fundamental truth of our social nature: our connections to others are essential to our well-being. Healing wasn't simply overcoming grief; it was about transforming it, finding strength in vulnerability, and celebrating the enduring power of love and human connection.

The journey wasn't easy. There were days when the weight of grief threatened to overwhelm me, days when the silence was deafening and the emptiness unbearable. But those days became less frequent, punctuated by moments of unexpected joy, of quiet contentment. I rediscovered the pleasure of a solitary walk in nature, the beauty of a sunset, the comfort of a good book. These weren't distractions from grief; they were acknowledgements of life's enduring beauty, a testament to the resilience of the human spirit.

The garden, always a source of shared joy for Connie and me, became my sanctuary. Tending to the roses, the lilies, the vibrant bursts of color that Connie loved so much, became a form of meditation, a connection to the life we had shared and a way of nurturing my own spirit. Each seed I planted, each blossom that unfolded, felt like a tiny victory, a symbol of renewal and growth. The garden, once a shared space, now became a place of solace, a tangible link to Connie's presence, a silent testament to our enduring love.

My friends, initially hesitant in their approach, became my unwavering support system. Their presence wasn't about fixing my grief; it was about acknowledging it, validating it, and sharing the simple joys of life that I had been unable to appreciate in the depths of my despair. Dinner parties, initially difficult, slowly became a source of comfort, a chance to reconnect with the world outside my grief, to laugh again, to share stories and memories. Their support wasn't merely about providing company; it was about allowing me to feel seen, heard, and loved, even in my vulnerability.

The legal battles, the fight for justice in the wake of Connie's death, became a focus, a way of channeling my anger and frustration into productive action. The process was arduous, emotionally draining, but it gave me a sense of purpose, a feeling of agency in a world that had felt utterly chaotic and out of control. It was a reminder that even in the midst of profound loss, we have the power to fight for what we believe in, to seek justice and accountability, even if the process is challenging and emotionally draining. The fight itself became part of my healing process, a way of honoring Connie's memory by ensuring that others wouldn't suffer the same injustice.

Engaging with spiritual practices deepened my understanding of grief, life, and death. The teachings of Lord Krishna, the wisdom of Chanakya, the quiet contemplation of nature—all provided a framework for understanding my grief, not as an ending, but as a part of life's cyclical nature. The concept of impermanence, so central to many spiritual traditions, helped me accept the reality of loss, to understand that grief is a natural part of the human experience, and that its intensity, while profound, is not permanent. Finding meaning in loss became a central part of my healing journey.

Rediscovering myself also meant engaging in new activities, in exploring interests that had been dormant during the years of intense focus on our shared life. I started painting, an art form that had always held a certain appeal but had been pushed aside. The vibrant colours, the act of creation, provided an outlet for my emotions, a way to express the joy and sadness, the anger and acceptance that filled my being. Each canvas became a reflection of my journey, a visual representation of my healing process, from the dark hues of early grief to the gradually emerging brighter, more hopeful colours.

Travel, once a cherished shared passion, slowly became a possibility again. Visiting places that held special memories with Connie provided a bittersweet reminder of our life together, but also offered a chance to reflect, to create new memories, and to discover new perspectives. Each trip, each new experience, was a step further away from the shadow of grief, a journey of self-discovery and renewal. The experiences, both positive and negative, became chapters in a new story, a story of resilience, adaptation, and the enduring power of the human spirit. It was a journey toward accepting the new reality of my life, a life without Connie, but also a life rich with possibility.

The process of rebuilding wasn't about replacing Connie; it was about creating space for a new chapter, a chapter that acknowledged the profound loss while embracing the possibilities of a future infused with purpose, meaning, and joy. The pain remains, a constant reminder of the love we shared, but it's no longer the defining force in my life. It's a part of me, woven into the fabric of my being, a constant reminder of the preciousness of life and the profound impact of human connection.

The journey continues. There are days when the grief resurfaces, when the memories are overwhelming, and the silence is deafening. But now, there are also days filled with laughter, contentment, and a renewed sense of purpose. I am no longer defined by my grief, but by my resilience, my ability to adapt, and my commitment to living a life worthy of the love we shared. The new beginnings are not erasing the past; rather, they are building upon it, creating a life that honors Connie's memory while embracing the possibilities of a future filled with joy, purpose, and a deep appreciation for the gift of life. The journey toward embracing new beginnings is ongoing, a testament to the enduring power of love, loss, and the indomitable human spirit. It is a journey that continues to evolve, a journey of growth, adaptation, and the discovery of a new normal, a normal that honors the past while embracing the hope and promise of the future. This is a new chapter, not a replacement, but a continuation, a testament to the enduring power of love and the resilience of the human heart. It's a chapter written not in despair, but in hope, in the quiet understanding that life, even after profound loss, can still be beautiful, meaningful, and profoundly fulfilling.

## Loves Resilience in the Face of Death

Death, the ultimate thief, had stolen Connie from me, leaving a void that seemed to swallow the very air I breathed. Forty-one years. Forty-one years of shared laughter, whispered secrets, and a love so profound it defied earthly comprehension. Forty-one years woven together, a tapestry of shared joys and sorrows, now ripped apart by a single, devastating thread. Yet, even as I navigated the treacherous currents of grief, something remained, a stubborn ember refusing to be extinguished: the enduring power of our love.

It wasn't a romanticized, saccharine notion. It wasn't the sentimental clinging to memories, although those were certainly precious. It was something deeper, more fundamental, a resonance that echoed in the silence, in the absence, a persistent hum beneath the surface of my unbearable pain. It was the knowledge, the unshakeable certainty, that the essence of Connie, the very core of who she was, was inextricably linked to mine. We had, as I believed, truly been two bodies, one soul. This belief, forged in the crucible of our shared life, became my anchor in the storm of grief.

The initial shock of her death had been brutal, a physical blow that left me gasping for air in a world suddenly devoid of oxygen. The world itself had lost its color, its vibrancy muted to a dull, monotonous gray. The routines we had shared, the unspoken rhythms of our days, were shattered. My mornings, once filled with the gentle sound of Connie humming in the kitchen, were now stark and lonely. Evenings, once spent in quiet conversation or engrossed in a shared book, stretched out before me, vast and empty. The

silence, once a comfort, had become a deafening roar, a
constant reminder of her absence.

My crisis management experience, honed over years of
navigating complex situations, proved unexpectedly useful.
It provided a framework, a structure to the chaos. I created a
daily routine, deliberately structuring my time with tasks,
however small, to give my days a semblance of order. It was
a battle against the overwhelming sense of purposelessness,
a conscious effort to rebuild a life that felt utterly
demolished.

Yet, amidst the practicalities of sorting her belongings, of
making funeral arrangements, of navigating the legal
complexities that followed, a different kind of work began.
The work of remembering. The work of reclaiming the
essence of our love. I delved into our photo albums, each
picture a tiny portal back to a moment of shared joy, a shared
laughter, a shared dream. I reread our letters, our emails,
each word a whisper from her across the chasm of death.

Our travels, our shared passion for exploring the world,
became vivid in my mind. I relived the sun-drenched
beaches of Santorini, the breathtaking majesty of the
Himalayas, the bustling markets of Marrakech. Each
journey, meticulously planned and executed together, was a
testament to our shared spirit, our ability to navigate the
unknown together. It wasn't just the physical places we
visited, but the shared experiences, the conversations, the
intimate moments of connection, that resonated now with an
even deeper poignancy.

Our love for art, for music, for literature, became a
sanctuary. I lost myself in the paintings we had admired
together, listening to the symphonies that had filled our
home with harmony. I revisited the novels we had discussed,

the poems that had sparked our imaginations. These shared passions, once a source of joy, now served as bridges across the chasm of grief, bringing me closer to Connie, even in her absence.

The anger, the searing rage over the alleged medical negligence that had contributed to her death, remained a powerful force. But it was not an anger that consumed me. It was an anger fueled by love, a determination to ensure that others wouldn't suffer the same loss, the same injustice. The legal battles were arduous, emotionally draining, but they were also a way of honoring Connie's memory, of fighting for the justice she deserved. It was a way of transforming my grief into action, into a purpose that extended beyond my personal pain.

As I delved deeper into my grief, I found solace in the teachings of Lord Krishna and Chanakya. Krishna's teachings on acceptance, on surrender to the divine will, provided a framework for understanding the inexplicability of loss. Chanakya's wisdom on justice, on the importance of duty, fueled my determination to seek accountability for Connie's death. These philosophical and spiritual insights weren't simply intellectual exercises; they became practical tools for navigating the complexities of grief, for finding meaning amidst the devastation.

The process of rebuilding my life, of rediscovering my identity outside the context of our shared existence, was slow and painstaking. It was a journey marked by setbacks and small victories, by moments of overwhelming despair and fleeting glimpses of hope. But throughout it all, the memory of Connie, the essence of our love, remained a constant source of strength, a guiding light in the darkness. It was not just the memory of specific events but the feeling, the profound connection, that persisted.

The enduring power of love, in the face of death, isn't about denying the pain, the loss, the overwhelming sense of emptiness. It's about acknowledging those feelings fully, embracing them, even as you hold onto the essence of the love that binds you, even beyond the grave. It's about transforming grief into gratitude, celebrating the life that was lived, cherishing the memories that remain. It's about keeping the flame of love alive, even in the darkest of nights, a testament to the enduring power of the human spirit, and the profound, unbreakable bond between two souls. It's about recognizing that the love we shared wasn't confined to the forty-one years we spent together on this earth; it transcends time, space, and even death itself. Connie may be gone from my physical world, but the love we shared, the essence of our bond, remains an integral part of who I am, a part of my very being, forever.

# Transforming Grief into Gratitude

The initial shock had subsided, replaced by a relentless ache, a hollowness that echoed in the silence of our once vibrant home. The vibrant colors of Connie's paintings seemed muted, the melodies of her favorite operas now sounded like mournful dirges. Each day was a struggle, a relentless climb up a steep, unforgiving incline. The world felt stark, stripped bare of its joy, its vibrancy. Yet, amidst this profound darkness, a tiny spark flickered. It was a faint ember of gratitude, a quiet whisper amidst the storm of grief.

It began subtly, in unexpected moments. The scent of jasmine, Connie's favorite, carried on a gentle breeze, evoked a flood of memories – her laughter, the warmth of her hand in mine, the quiet intimacy of our shared evenings. It wasn't a denial of my pain; it was an acknowledgment of the immeasurable beauty that had once been, a recognition of the gift of our forty-one years together. This gratitude wasn't a forced sentiment, a superficial attempt to overcome my grief. It was an organic process, a gradual unfolding, like a flower pushing its way through hardened earth.

I started to keep a journal, not to wallow in sorrow, but to document the memories, the moments of joy, the shared experiences that had shaped our lives. Each entry became a small act of defiance against the despair, a testament to the richness of our shared history. I would write about our travels – the breathtaking sunsets in Santorini, the bustling markets of Marrakech, the serene beauty of the Japanese gardens. I'd recall the countless evenings spent discussing philosophy, debating politics, sharing our dreams and aspirations. I would remember the quiet moments of intimacy, the shared laughter, the unspoken understanding that bound us together. These weren't simply recollections; they were acts of remembrance, a way of keeping Connie alive in my heart, even as her physical presence was gone.

My professional background in crisis management oddly proved invaluable during this time. I knew the importance of structured coping mechanisms, of finding healthy outlets for my emotions. But this wasn't just about technical strategies; it was about nurturing a genuine sense of gratitude for the life we had shared. Grief, I realized, wasn't just about loss; it was also about legacy. Connie had left an indelible mark on the world, on me, on everyone who knew her. And that legacy deserved to be celebrated, not mourned.

This realization spurred me to seek out ways to honor her memory. I started volunteering at the local art center, a place Connie had dearly loved. I donated to charities that supported causes close to her heart, organizations dedicated to alleviating poverty and promoting education. Each act was a small step, a way of transforming my grief into a positive force, a means of channeling my sorrow into something meaningful and constructive. It was a way of saying, "Connie, your life mattered, and I will continue to live in a way that honors your memory and the values we shared."

The spiritual and philosophical perspectives I'd long embraced now offered a deeper understanding of my grief. The teachings of Lord Krishna, with his emphasis on acceptance and detachment, provided solace. The wisdom of Chanakya, with his focus on duty and righteousness, gave me the strength to persevere. I realized that death was not an end but a transition, a passage into another realm. Connie's essence, her spirit, wasn't confined to her physical body; it lived on in the memories we shared, in the love that bound us, in the impact she had on the world. And that realization filled me with a deep sense of peace.

My anger over the alleged medical negligence that had contributed to Connie's death remained, a potent force that fueled my determination to seek justice. This wasn't simply about personal revenge; it was about holding those responsible accountable, ensuring that others wouldn't suffer the same fate. The fight for justice became another channel for my grief, a way of honoring Connie's memory by preventing similar tragedies. This fight, however challenging, became a testament to the enduring strength of my love for her, a manifestation of my commitment to ensuring that her death wasn't in vain.

But justice alone wasn't enough. I needed more than simply retribution. I needed to find healing, to integrate my grief into the fabric of my life, to transform it into something beautiful and meaningful. This was where the power of gratitude truly came into play. It wasn't about forgetting Connie; it was about remembering her in a way that celebrated her life, her spirit, and the profound love we had shared.

I started appreciating the small things, the simple joys that I had once taken for granted. The warmth of the sun on my skin, the beauty of a blooming flower, the quiet comfort of a cup of tea – these were moments of gratitude, reminders of the beauty that still existed in the world, even amidst my profound loss. I started noticing the kindness of strangers, the support of my friends and family. These acts of compassion became sources of strength, helping me navigate the turbulent waters of grief.

The transformative power of gratitude extended beyond my personal healing. It became a source of inspiration for others struggling with loss. I started sharing my experiences, my reflections, in small groups and online forums. It was surprising how many people resonated with my story, how many found solace in my journey of transforming grief into gratitude. The act of sharing my pain, my struggles, and my eventual healing, became a source of strength, not only for myself but for others who were grappling with their own losses.

The process wasn't linear; there were days when the grief felt overwhelming, when the pain threatened to consume me. But the embers of gratitude, though sometimes faint, always remained. They were like beacons in the darkness, guiding me toward a path of healing, a path of acceptance, a path that allowed me to honor Connie's memory while simultaneously embracing the future. The enduring power of our love wasn't just a sentimental notion; it was a tangible force that shaped my life, even in the face of unimaginable loss.

The journey of transforming grief into gratitude wasn't about erasing the pain; it was about integrating it into the tapestry of my life, acknowledging its profound impact while simultaneously celebrating the beauty and richness of the life we had shared. It was about finding meaning in loss, discovering strength in vulnerability, and embracing a future where Connie's memory continues to inspire and guide me. It's a journey I continue to walk, each step a testament to the enduring power of love and the transformative power of gratitude.

The legal battle continued, demanding time and energy, but it no longer consumed me entirely. The focus shifted, becoming a parallel path to the journey of healing. The pursuit of justice became a tribute, a way to ensure that no one else experienced the kind of medical negligence that Connie had faced. Each step towards accountability became a small victory, not only in the legal sense, but also in my personal journey of transforming grief into meaningful action.

The anniversaries of Connie's passing were initially unbearable, each one a fresh wave of grief. However, gradually, these dates became opportunities for reflection and celebration. I would visit her favorite places, revisit cherished memories, and share stories of our life together with loved ones. The pain remained, but it was interwoven with gratitude—gratitude for the life we shared, the love we experienced, the memories we created.

Over time, the emptiness started to lessen, replaced by a quiet acceptance. The void wasn't completely filled, but it was no longer a gaping chasm, swallowing me whole. It was more like a gentle hollow, a space where Connie's memory resided, a reminder of her presence in my life, a testament to the enduring power of our bond.

The transformation wasn't a miraculous overnight cure; it was a gradual process, a slow, deliberate unfolding. It involved confronting the raw pain, allowing myself to grieve, but also actively seeking out moments of gratitude, celebrating the memories, and focusing on the positive impact Connie had on the world and on me. The path from grief to gratitude was long and winding, filled with ups and downs, moments of despair and moments of unexpected joy.

And so, the narrative unfolds – a journey of loss, yes, but also a testament to the transformative power of love, the strength of the human spirit, and the surprising grace that can emerge even from the depths of despair. It is a story of healing, not forgetting, but transforming the pain into a legacy of gratitude, a profound appreciation for the life that was, and a commitment to living a life worthy of the love shared. It is a story of two souls, bound together even beyond the boundaries of death.

## Celebrating a Life WellLived

The initial numbness had begun to recede, replaced by a more insidious pain – the gnawing ache of absence. Yet, even in the depths of my sorrow, a quiet revolution was taking place within me. It wasn't a sudden shift, but a gradual dawning, a slow and deliberate turning towards the light. I began to understand that while my heart was broken, Connie's life was not. Her legacy, her vibrant spirit, continued to resonate, a powerful counterpoint to the silence that had enveloped our home. This wasn't simply about remembering; it was about celebrating. It was about honoring the remarkable woman who had shared my life for over four decades.

Connie wasn't just my wife; she was a force of nature, a whirlwind of creativity, intelligence, and unwavering kindness. Her laughter was infectious, her spirit indomitable. She approached life with a passion that was both inspiring and humbling. Her artistic talent was undeniable, her paintings bursting with color, emotion, and a deep understanding of the human condition. Each canvas told a story, a testament to her perceptive eye and skillful hand. I remember the countless hours we spent in galleries, museums, and art studios, our conversations flowing as freely as the paint on her palette. These weren't just visits; they were pilgrimages, shared explorations of beauty and meaning.

Beyond her artistic gifts, Connie possessed a sharp intellect, a keen mind that constantly sought knowledge and understanding. She devoured books like a starving person consuming a feast, her curiosity insatiable. Our discussions were often lively debates, fueled by our shared passion for philosophy, history, and literature. We'd spend hours dissecting the intricacies of ancient scriptures, exploring the complexities of human behavior, and debating the merits of different schools of thought. These intellectual exchanges were the cornerstone of our bond, enriching our lives in ways I'm only beginning to fully comprehend.

Her commitment to social justice was another defining characteristic. She wasn't content to simply observe injustice; she actively worked to combat it. She volunteered at numerous charities, advocating for the marginalized and the vulnerable. Her compassion was boundless, her empathy unwavering. I recall her tireless efforts to raise awareness about environmental issues, her unwavering belief in the power of collective action. She was a champion for the underdog, a voice for the voiceless. Her legacy extends far beyond our personal lives; it's woven into the fabric of the community she loved and served so faithfully.

Beyond the intellectual and artistic pursuits, Connie's life was a tapestry woven with threads of simple joys and everyday miracles. She had a remarkable ability to find beauty in the mundane, to appreciate the small things that often go unnoticed. A sunrise, a blooming flower, a child's laughter – she saw the divine in every detail. Her ability to find joy in the simple things was a constant source of inspiration, a reminder to cherish the moments, the quiet moments of shared intimacy, the gentle caress of a hand, the warm embrace of love. These are the memories that sustain me, the quiet echoes of a life lived fully, a life brimming with love and grace.

Her culinary skills were another testament to her generosity and love. Our kitchen was often filled with the aroma of exotic spices and simmering sauces, the result of her culinary adventures. She could transform the simplest ingredients into culinary masterpieces, her meals a celebration of flavors and textures. These weren't just meals; they were acts of love, expressions of her devotion and care. Sharing these meals together, surrounded by friends and family, were some of the most cherished moments of our life together. They represent more than sustenance; they embody the warmth and connection that defined our marriage.

Connie's influence extended to all aspects of our lives, shaping my perspectives, challenging my assumptions, and expanding my horizons. She was my confidante, my advisor, my greatest supporter. She believed in me even when I doubted myself, encouraged me to pursue my dreams even when the path seemed daunting. She was my anchor, my safe harbor, the one constant in a world of ever-changing tides. Her faith in me was unwavering, a testament to the depth of our connection. The loss of this unwavering support is a wound that will take time to heal, a gap that will never truly be filled.

But the memories, the echoes of her laughter, the warmth of her touch, the wisdom of her words – these remain. And they are not just remnants of the past; they are the building blocks of my future. I am learning to carry her legacy forward, to honor her memory by living a life that is worthy of the love we shared. I am learning to find peace not in forgetting, but in remembering – in celebrating the extraordinary life of an extraordinary woman. The pain is still raw, the void still profound, but I am gradually finding my way through the darkness, guided by the enduring light of her love.

The outpouring of love and support from friends and family after Connie's passing was immense, a testament to the impact she had on so many lives. It was both comforting and overwhelming – a constant reminder of the powerful connections she had forged, the bonds of friendship and love she had nurtured. Letters and cards poured in, each one a precious artifact, a piece of a larger mosaic portraying the depth of her character and the breadth of her influence. These testimonials reaffirmed what I already knew: Connie's life was far more than just mine; it was a gift to the world.

Her influence extended beyond our immediate circle. Many shared stories of how Connie's kindness, her wisdom, or even her casual act of compassion had profoundly impacted their lives. These stories, both large and small, illustrated a pattern of generosity and selflessness that reflected her true nature. She touched countless lives in subtle and profound ways, leaving behind a legacy of kindness that continues to inspire. This realization, born out of grief, has ironically become a source of profound solace.

In seeking justice for the perceived medical negligence that contributed to Connie's death, I stumbled upon an unexpected side effect – a renewed appreciation for the importance of transparency and accountability within the healthcare system. My quest for answers was not simply a personal one; it became a mission to advocate for improved standards and ethical practices. Connie's passing, though intensely painful, unexpectedly fueled a new purpose – a commitment to preventing similar tragedies from happening to others. This newfound purpose, while born out of loss, has become a powerful source of healing and a testament to the enduring strength of her spirit.

The anger and frustration I felt in the initial aftermath of Connie's passing slowly gave way to a more profound understanding. It wasn't simply about apportioning blame or seeking retribution. It was about learning from the experience, about seeking positive change. The legal battle, though emotionally draining, ultimately led to a reevaluation of my own priorities and a deeper commitment to making a meaningful contribution to society. It became a way to honor Connie's memory – not through dwelling on the negative, but by striving to create something positive in the face of immense loss.

Through the process of writing this memoir, of chronicling our lives together, I've discovered a new way to connect with Connie – not just through memory, but through the act of creation. The act of writing itself has become a form of therapy, a means of processing the complex emotions of grief and loss. Each word, each sentence, is a small step forward, a small act of healing. In recounting our journey, I have not only honored her memory but also discovered a deeper understanding of myself, of our relationship, and of the meaning of a life well-lived.

And in celebrating Connie's life, I am also celebrating the enduring power of love. It's a love that transcends death, a love that continues to shape my life, to guide my decisions, to inspire my actions. It is a love that is not extinguished by loss, but rather transmuted, refined, and deepened by the experience of grief. The love we shared wasn't simply a feeling; it was a commitment, a promise, a bond that extends beyond the physical realm. It is a testament to the power of two souls, intertwined, inseparable, even in the face of death. And that, perhaps, is the most enduring legacy of all. The profound and unshakeable feeling that even in the face of absolute despair, love conquers all. A love that resonates beyond the physical, a love that echoes through time and eternity. A love that, in its own way, helps us find meaning even when the world feels meaningless. A love that, ultimately, enables us to celebrate a life well-lived, a life overflowing with love, laughter, and an unwavering commitment to making a positive impact on the world. A life that continues to inspire and uplift even in its absence.

## Keeping Memories Alive

The silence in the house was a constant companion, a stark contrast to the vibrant tapestry of our forty-one years together. Connie's absence echoed in every room, in every corner, a void that seemed impossible to fill. Yet, amidst the grief, a quiet determination took root. I wouldn't let her memory fade; I wouldn't allow the vibrant tapestry of our life together to unravel. Keeping Connie's memory alive became a sacred duty, a testament to the enduring power of our love.

My initial approach was almost frantic, a desperate attempt to cling to the tangible remnants of our shared life. I meticulously sorted through her belongings, each item a poignant reminder of moments shared, laughter exchanged, dreams realized. Her wardrobe, filled with clothes that reflected her impeccable style and vibrant personality, became a silent museum, each garment a story waiting to be told. Her jewelry, each piece a gift or a memento of a special occasion, sparkled with memories, each reflecting a unique chapter in our life's narrative. Her books, lined up on the shelves, stood as silent witnesses to our shared intellectual adventures, our countless hours spent discussing philosophy, history, and literature. Even her gardening tools, resting in the shed, spoke volumes about her love for nature, her ability to nurture life, to bring beauty into existence.

But simply preserving her belongings wasn't enough. It was a passive act, a melancholic cataloging of the past. I needed an active process, a dynamic way to keep her spirit alive, to keep her laughter echoing in the corridors of my memory. I began by creating a digital archive, carefully scanning photographs, letters, and documents. I assembled hundreds of images, chronicling our life together, from our courtship to our later years. Each photograph was more than just a snapshot; it was a portal to a specific memory, a vibrant scene from our shared narrative. I painstakingly labelled and categorized each image, creating a visual chronicle of our journey together. I spent countless hours meticulously crafting detailed descriptions, adding context and anecdotes to each picture, transforming them into living memories, preserving not just the images but the very essence of those moments.

Beyond the digital archive, I started a journal, a dedicated space to pour out my thoughts, my reflections, my memories of Connie. It became a sanctuary, a place where I could freely express my grief, my anger, my longing, without fear of judgment or constraint. The pages were filled with both painful recollections and joyful reminiscences, a raw and unfiltered account of my emotional landscape. I wrote about our travels, our shared passions, our intellectual debates, our laughter, our tears – a complete tapestry of our lives woven together with words. This was more than just a journal; it was a testament to the depth and richness of our bond, a living memorial to a life well-lived.

Furthermore, I decided to create a physical album, a tangible representation of our love story. I selected some of our most cherished photographs and meticulously arranged them, accompanied by handwritten captions and anecdotes. The album was not merely a collection of pictures; it was a curated narrative, a meticulously crafted story of our life together, a testament to the enduring power of our love. Each page spoke of a specific event, a shared dream, a moment of profound connection, bringing her back to life, transforming those images into living memories. The tactile experience of holding the album, turning its pages, and tracing my fingers over the photographs provided a profound sense of connection to Connie. It became a sacred object, cherished and reverently handled, a treasure that allowed me to reconnect with her in a deeply personal and meaningful way.

Then came the idea of sharing Connie's story, not just with myself but with others. I began writing this book, "Two Bodies & One Soul," as a way to process my grief, to make sense of my loss, to celebrate Connie's life, and to ensure her legacy would endure. The act of writing became a form of therapy, a way to channel my emotions, to give voice to my pain, and ultimately, to transform my grief into a celebration of our love. It was a cathartic experience, a journey of self-discovery and healing. I poured all my love, all my pain, all my memories into these pages, hoping to share the extraordinary woman Connie was with the world.

The journey of keeping Connie's memory alive wasn't merely a sentimental exercise; it was an act of justice, a profound way of honoring her life and resisting the insidious encroachment of oblivion. It required a conscious and consistent effort, a dedicated pursuit that became intertwined with my healing process. It's a process of remembrance and reclamation, of preserving the tapestry of our shared life, ensuring that the vibrant colors of our love story wouldn't fade. This wasn't about preserving things but about preserving the spirit of a remarkable woman, a beautiful soul, who made my life profoundly meaningful.

Beyond the physical artifacts, I also sought to preserve Connie's legacy in other ways. I contacted her friends and colleagues, collecting anecdotes and stories that enriched my understanding of her life and personality. These recollections filled in gaps in my own memory, revealing aspects of her character and life that I hadn't fully appreciated. Each story added another layer of depth to my understanding of Connie, enriching my personal narrative and allowing me to build a more complete picture of the woman I loved. These memories, recounted by those who knew her best, revealed a different dimension of Connie's personality, a collection of perspectives that further enriched my appreciation for her life.

Moreover, I actively sought to continue activities and pursuits that we shared. Our love for travel, for instance, found a new expression. Though it felt different now, travelling alone to places we once explored together provided a poignant connection to our past. Each location brought back vivid memories, allowing me to relive the experience, sharing those moments in my mind with Connie, revisiting those landscapes together, as if our spirits were once again traveling side-by-side. It was a bittersweet experience, but a powerful reminder of our shared adventures and a way of keeping her memory alive. The same principle applied to our shared love for the arts and intellectual pursuits; each visit to a museum, each book I read, each philosophical debate I engaged in, served as a link to her, maintaining the vibrant connections that had always defined our relationship.

The pain of losing Connie was, and continues to be, immense. But even in the darkest moments, the enduring power of our love, the depth of our shared life, sustains me. It is a love that transcends death, a love that continues to shape my life, to guide my decisions, and to inspire my actions. It's a love that transcends the realm of feelings; it's a profound commitment, a promise, a bond that extends far beyond the confines of time and space. It's a legacy I intend to honor, not only through remembrance but also through living a life worthy of the love we shared, a life that will continue to reflect the values and principles we held dear. This commitment is a testament to the unique destiny we shared, a profound testament to the enduring power of a love that knows no bounds.

The process of keeping Connie's memory alive is a continual journey, a lifelong commitment. It's a dynamic process, evolving and adapting as time unfolds. It's not a linear process; it's filled with ups and downs, moments of profound joy intertwined with moments of intense sorrow. But each moment, each memory, each act of remembrance strengthens the enduring bond that binds us, a testament to a love that transcends the boundaries of life and death. The depth of our connection is a source of both immense sorrow and profound comfort. It's a reminder of the beautiful life we shared, the unique journey we undertook together, and the immeasurable impact she had on my life.

Keeping her memory alive is not just about preserving the past; it's about shaping the future. It's about carrying forward the values we cherished, the dreams we shared, the principles we believed in. It's about living a life that honors our shared commitment, reflecting the beautiful legacy she left behind. It's a life that would make her proud, a life guided by love, justice, and a profound respect for the life we shared. Connie's memory is not a static entity; it's a living, breathing presence that continues to shape my life, my actions, and my aspirations. It is a powerful testament to the enduring power of love, even in the face of unimaginable loss. It is a love that sustains me, guides me, and inspires me to live a life that honors her memory and the beautiful life we shared. It's a love that continues to define my existence, long after her physical presence has faded from this world. And in that, I find solace, strength, and the unwavering conviction to continue celebrating her life. The journey of remembrance is a continuous process, a testament to a love story that transcends time itself.

## The Legacy of Love

The quiet hum of the refrigerator, a sound once barely noticeable amidst the symphony of our lives, now grated on my nerves. It was a constant reminder of the emptiness, the chilling absence. Yet, amidst this profound sorrow, a different kind of energy stirred within me – a quiet resolve, a determination forged in the crucible of grief. Connie's legacy wasn't merely the sum of our shared memories, but a living, breathing force that shaped my present and would guide my future. It was a legacy I was committed to upholding, not as a passive observer but as an active participant in its ongoing narrative.

Our forty-one years together were not simply a collection of moments; they were a tapestry woven with threads of shared dreams, unwavering commitment, and a deep, abiding love that transcended the boundaries of space and time. Connie's influence was subtle yet pervasive, resonating in every decision I made, every path I chose. Her laughter, her wisdom, her indomitable spirit – these weren't just memories to be cherished, but guiding principles that illuminated my way forward.

One of the most profound aspects of Connie's legacy was her unwavering dedication to justice. She possessed a keen sense of right and wrong, an unwavering belief in fairness, and a powerful empathy for the marginalized. This wasn't a mere intellectual position; it was a deeply ingrained part of her being, reflected in her actions, her choices, and her unwavering support for causes she believed in. Her influence extended beyond our immediate family; she actively championed the rights of the underprivileged, donating her time and resources to charitable causes. This passion for justice was a flame she ignited within me, a commitment I now carry forward with a renewed sense of purpose. Her legacy compels me to fight for fairness, to speak up against injustice, and to continue the fight for a more equitable world, a world she so deeply desired.

Another vital thread in Connie's legacy was her profound love for learning. She devoured books with insatiable curiosity, her mind a vibrant garden constantly blooming with new knowledge and understanding. She wasn't merely a consumer of information; she was a passionate seeker of truth, constantly questioning assumptions and challenging conventional wisdom. This intellectual curiosity extended to all aspects of her life, from her keen interest in philosophy and spirituality to her meticulous attention to detail in her artistic pursuits. She taught me the importance of lifelong learning, the value of intellectual humility, and the profound satisfaction that comes from continuous growth and exploration. Her library, once a haven of shared discovery, now serves as a poignant reminder of her intellect and her relentless pursuit of knowledge. I continue to explore the books she loved, finding solace and inspiration in the pages she once turned. It's a way to keep her spirit alive, to continue our intellectual journey, even in her absence.

Her love for art, particularly painting, was another facet of her enduring legacy. Her canvases, now carefully preserved, are not merely works of art but windows into her soul, vibrant expressions of her creativity, her emotions, and her deep connection to the world around her. Each brushstroke tells a story, a testament to her artistic passion and her ability to translate her inner world onto the canvas. Looking at her paintings, I feel her presence, her spirit, her passion. They are not static images; they are living memories, constantly shifting and changing with my own emotional landscape. They are a testament to the vibrant soul that once graced our lives, a soul that continues to inspire and motivate me. I find comfort in preserving her artistic legacy, ensuring her work continues to inspire and bring joy to others. I plan exhibitions, share her works digitally, and engage with artists who share her vision to keep her artistic flame burning brightly.

Beyond her individual passions, Connie's legacy extended to our shared values, our shared life, and the principles we held dear. Our travels, our shared laughter, our intimate conversations – these were not just moments in time, but building blocks of a love story that transcended the boundaries of the physical world. We created a life rich in experiences, a tapestry of memories that will forever remain etched in my heart. Even in the face of unimaginable loss, the memories of our shared adventures, the quiet moments of intimacy, the joyous celebrations, and the comforting presence of her hand in mine remain vivid and potent. These shared experiences are not merely recollections of the past; they are the foundation upon which I continue to build my life. They are a testament to the enduring strength of our bond, a bond that transcends time and space, a bond that continues to nourish and sustain me.

Connie's legacy is not solely defined by grand gestures or monumental achievements. It's found in the subtle nuances of her character, in her kindness, her empathy, her unwavering integrity. Her legacy is in the quiet moments, the gentle smiles, the acts of selfless love. It is in the way she made me a better person, in the way she encouraged my dreams, in the way she celebrated my triumphs, and in the way she supported me through my struggles. Her legacy is woven into the fabric of my being, shaping my thoughts, my actions, and my aspirations. It is a legacy I carry within me, a constant reminder of the profound love we shared and the enduring impact she had on my life.

The journey of grief is not a linear path; it's a winding road, filled with unexpected turns and unforeseen challenges. There are days when the pain is almost unbearable, days when the silence screams louder than any sound. Yet, even in the darkest moments, Connie's legacy shines as a beacon of hope, reminding me of the beauty and strength of the love we shared. It's a love that transcends the boundaries of life and death, a love that continues to inspire me, a love that sustains me even in the face of profound loss.

In the pursuit of justice regarding the alleged medical negligence that contributed to Connie's passing, I found another outlet for my grief. It wasn't just a legal battle; it was a fight to honor her memory, to prevent others from suffering a similar fate. This determination wasn't born out of vengeance, but out of a deep-seated belief in justice and a profound commitment to ensuring accountability. The legal process was arduous, often frustrating, but it provided a framework for channeling my grief into productive action. It was a testament to Connie's spirit, her unwavering belief in fairness, and her passionate commitment to justice for all.

Through the process of writing this book, of recounting our story, of exploring the depths of my grief, I've discovered a new understanding of love's enduring power. It's not merely a feeling, a fleeting emotion; it's a force, a life-shaping energy that transcends time and space. Connie's love continues to shape my life, guiding my decisions, inspiring my actions, and providing solace in the face of overwhelming sorrow. It's a love that gives me strength, that fuels my determination, that sustains me. It's a love that continues to grow and evolve, even in the absence of its physical embodiment.

The concept of "two bodies and one soul" has taken on a deeper significance for me. While her physical body is gone, her soul, her essence, remains intrinsically linked to mine. I feel her presence in the quiet moments, in the rustling leaves, in the gentle breeze. It's a connection that transcends the limitations of the physical world, a connection that continues to sustain and nourish me. This intimate connection, this enduring bond, is the heart of Connie's legacy, a legacy I will continue to honor, cherish, and celebrate for as long as I live. It's a commitment that permeates every aspect of my life, a commitment to living a life worthy of the love we shared, a life that honors her memory, and a life that reflects the beautiful legacy she left behind. The legacy of love is not an ending, but a continuation, a transformative journey, a testament to the indomitable spirit of a love that knows no bounds. It's a love that continues to shape my future, a love that defines my present, a love that guides my every step, a love that will forever remain the cornerstone of my existence.

And as I look to the future, I find strength and purpose in the memory of our shared life, in the lessons she taught me, and in the legacy of love that she so generously bestowed upon me. It is a legacy that I will strive to honor, not just through words, but through actions, through a life lived with integrity, compassion, and a relentless pursuit of justice. It's a legacy that will continue to shape and inspire me, long after the last page of this book is turned. The love we shared wasn't merely a chapter in my life; it is the foundation upon which my future is built. It's a legacy that extends beyond the confines of this book, a legacy that will continue to resonate, to inspire, and to guide me towards a future that honors the profound love we shared and the enduring power of a love that transcends the boundaries of life and death. It is a love that will forever remain a beacon of hope, a source of strength, and a guiding light on my life's journey.

# The Role of Greed in Healthcare

The insidious tendrils of greed have long infiltrated the sanctity of healthcare, twisting its noble purpose into a grotesque parody of compassion and care. This is not merely a matter of individual avarice; it's a systemic issue, a cancerous growth that metastasizes through the very fabric of our medical systems, impacting every level, from the boardroom to the bedside. Connie's case, tragically, became a stark illustration of this pervasive problem. While the immediate failures involved specific individuals and their negligence, a deeper examination reveals a far more troubling truth: a system where profit often outweighs patient well-being, where shortcuts are taken, and corners are cut in the pursuit of financial gain.

The pharmaceutical industry, a behemoth of power and influence, stands accused, and often rightly so. The exorbitant pricing of life-saving drugs, the aggressive marketing of unnecessary treatments, and the lobbying efforts to stifle competition—these actions are not the isolated acts of rogue actors but rather symptoms of a deeply entrenched system prioritizing profit maximization above all else. The cost of developing new drugs is undeniably high, but the markups applied to many medications are simply unconscionable. This inflated pricing drives up healthcare costs, making essential treatments inaccessible to millions, particularly those without robust insurance coverage. It forces difficult choices: treatment or rent, medication or food. This is a moral failing of epic proportions.

Furthermore, the profit motive pervades medical practices themselves. The pressure to maximize billable hours, to schedule more patients than can be adequately cared for, and to prioritize lucrative procedures over preventative care, creates a climate where genuine patient needs are often secondary to financial incentives. Doctors, often burdened by immense student loan debt and pressured by administrative demands, can find themselves trapped in a system that incentivizes volume over quality. The system, it seems, is designed to reward those who generate the most revenue, not those who provide the best care. This creates a perverse incentive structure that ultimately harms patients.

The story of Connie's illness, and the subsequent accusations of medical negligence, is not unique. Countless similar tragedies occur daily, each a testament to the failures inherent in a system that has prioritized profit over people. These failures are not simply the result of individual incompetence or negligence; they are a consequence of a systemic problem where the pursuit of profit often overshadows the fundamental ethical obligations of healthcare providers. The relentless pressure to increase revenue often leads to understaffing, overworked healthcare professionals, and a lack of investment in proper equipment and training. This contributes to a cascade of errors, leading to misdiagnosis, delayed treatment, and preventable medical harm.

Consider the stories of countless patients who have been denied necessary treatment due to high costs, who have endured long waits for appointments, who have suffered due to poorly trained staff, or who have been subjected to unnecessary procedures purely for financial reasons. These are not isolated incidents but rather common occurrences within a flawed system. The pressure to meet financial targets can also lead to a prioritization of speed and efficiency over careful attention to detail. Rushed procedures and poorly executed diagnostics are, sadly, all too common, contributing significantly to medical errors.

The sheer volume of medical malpractice lawsuits filed each year serves as a grim indicator of the extent of this problem. While not every lawsuit is justified, the sheer number highlights a pervasive issue within healthcare that needs addressing. The system is not self-correcting; the pursuit of profit often obfuscates responsibility and creates obstacles to accountability. Often, institutions prioritize protecting their reputation and financial interests over acknowledging and rectifying their errors. This culture of silence and avoidance of accountability allows negligent practices to continue unabated, resulting in further suffering for patients and their families.

My experience in crisis management has taught me the critical importance of swift, decisive action in the face of adversity. In the case of Connie's illness and subsequent death, the lack of transparency, the deflection of responsibility, and the slow, agonizing process of seeking justice left an enduring scar. The system seemed designed to protect itself rather than to acknowledge and rectify the mistakes that had cost Connie her life. This is not merely a matter of individual negligence, but a systemic failure rooted in a prioritization of profit over human life.

Beyond the individual tragedies, the systemic failures within healthcare have broader societal implications. The erosion of trust in healthcare providers, the inequities in access to care, and the soaring costs of medical treatment are all direct consequences of prioritizing profit over people. These problems are not easily solved, but acknowledging their existence is the critical first step toward meaningful reform. There needs to be a fundamental shift in the culture of healthcare, a re-prioritization of values that places the well-being of patients above all other considerations. This requires regulatory oversight, robust accountability mechanisms, and a societal commitment to ensuring access to affordable, high-quality healthcare for all.

The fight for justice in Connie's case was, in many ways, a fight against this deeply entrenched system. It was a struggle against the forces of greed and indifference that had allowed negligence to flourish. While the legal battles were challenging and emotionally draining, the fight was not solely for personal closure. It was also a fight for systemic change, a fight to hold the healthcare industry accountable for its failures, and a fight to prevent similar tragedies from happening to others.

The experience has profoundly changed my perspective on healthcare, revealing a world where the pursuit of profit often eclipses the inherent humanity of medicine. The callous disregard for human life, the prioritization of financial gain over patient welfare, and the systemic failures to provide accountability have left an indelible mark. But out of this profound grief and anger, a resolve has emerged—a commitment to advocating for systemic reform, for greater transparency, and for a healthcare system that truly values human life above all else. Connie's memory serves as a powerful reminder of the human cost of greed and negligence, and fuels my ongoing commitment to ensuring that others do not suffer the same fate. Her legacy is not just a story of loss, but also a call to action, a demand for change. The fight for justice, for a better healthcare system, continues.

## Systemic Failures and Accountability

The initial shock of Connie's death, the raw, visceral pain of loss, gradually gave way to a chilling understanding. It wasn't simply a matter of individual negligence; it was a systemic failure, a cascade of errors facilitated by a system designed, it seemed, to prioritize profit over patient care. The insidious nature of this realization gnawed at me, fueling a righteous anger that continues to burn even now. It wasn't enough to grieve; I needed to understand, to expose the rot that allowed such a tragedy to unfold.

My background in crisis management, though seemingly unrelated to the intimate tragedy of losing my wife, provided a framework for dissecting the sequence of events leading to Connie's death. I began meticulously collecting medical records, scrutinizing every test result, every consultation note, every interaction with medical personnel. The sheer volume of information was overwhelming, a dense thicket of technical jargon and medical terminology. Yet, as I painstakingly pieced together the narrative, a disturbing pattern emerged.

Early detection of Connie's cancer was missed due to a combination of factors. The initial symptoms, subtle and easily dismissed, were overlooked by a physician preoccupied with meeting patient quotas rather than meticulously assessing each case. This, I learned, wasn't an isolated incident. The pressure to maintain high patient volume, coupled with inadequate compensation, created an environment where thoroughness and attentiveness were sacrificed at the altar of efficiency. This was not a flaw within a single practitioner; it was an inherent flaw in the model itself. The compensation structure incentivized speed over quality, a dangerous formula in the field of medicine. The consequences were fatal.

Further compounding the issue, the diagnostic imaging equipment at the clinic was outdated and prone to inaccuracies. Maintenance had been deferred due to budgetary constraints, highlighting a systemic problem of underfunding within healthcare facilities. It wasn't simply a lack of resources; it was a deliberate decision to prioritize short-term cost savings over long-term patient safety. This spoke volumes about the misplaced priorities of the institution. Profit, it seemed, reigned supreme.

The subsequent treatment also revealed disturbing flaws. The oncologist, while seemingly competent, was burdened by an unmanageable patient load, leading to rushed consultations and oversight of crucial details. The communication between specialists was inadequate, critical information lost in the bureaucratic maze of medical paperwork. Again, this wasn't the fault of a single individual acting out of malice. It was a system that was inherently overburdened, understaffed, and under-resourced, creating an environment rife for errors and miscommunication. The system failed Connie, not merely through negligence, but through structural inadequacy.

My research led me to discover a shocking prevalence of similar cases. I began to connect with other families who had experienced comparable medical tragedies. Their stories mirrored Connie's, a horrifying chorus of missed diagnoses, delayed treatment, and inadequate care, all stemming from the same systemic failures. These weren't isolated incidents; they were symptoms of a deeply flawed healthcare system.

The conversations with these families provided a sense of shared pain, a solidarity born out of shared loss. But more importantly, they confirmed my suspicions. This wasn't about bad apples; it was a rotten barrel. The healthcare system, in its current form, was susceptible to greed and negligence at every level, from the boardroom to the bedside. This realization solidified my determination to pursue accountability.

But the path to accountability was fraught with obstacles. The legal system, designed to protect individuals, seemed ill-equipped to grapple with the complex web of systemic failures. Lawsuits often focus on individual negligence, overlooking the broader systemic issues that contribute to medical errors. Furthermore, the powerful institutions involved had significant resources to fight back, often employing legal strategies designed to delay, obfuscate, and ultimately avoid responsibility.

This experience highlighted the critical need for transparency within the healthcare industry. The lack of accountability in the face of medical error is deeply troubling. It creates an environment of impunity, where institutions are more concerned with protecting their reputation and avoiding liability than with ensuring patient safety. This is an outrage; it violates the very core principles of patient care.

My efforts to secure justice for Connie, to hold those responsible accountable, became a mission. It was a battle against not only individual negligence but also against a system that prioritizes profit over patient care. This fight fueled by grief and fueled by the sheer injustice of it all, became a powerful catalyst for change. It was a journey that transformed personal grief into a determination to create a healthcare system more focused on empathy, compassion and patient safety.

The pursuit of accountability revealed the deeply entrenched nature of systemic failures within healthcare. Financial incentives, bureaucratic inertia, and a culture of silence often hindered effective investigation and meaningful change. Regulatory bodies, while intended to protect patients, sometimes lacked the resources or the will to effectively oversee the healthcare industry. The result is a system where patients are vulnerable, and the pursuit of profit often eclipses the fundamental values of ethical healthcare.

The experience profoundly altered my perspective on the concept of justice. It's not enough to hold individual actors responsible; we must address the systemic issues that enable negligence and greed to flourish. This requires a multi-pronged approach, encompassing regulatory reforms, increased transparency, and a cultural shift within the healthcare industry.

The fight for a better healthcare system is a marathon, not a sprint. It demands sustained effort, vigilance, and a commitment to holding institutions accountable for their actions. It requires a fundamental shift in priorities, placing patient well-being above profit motives. Only then can we hope to prevent future tragedies like Connie's.

The lessons learned from this painful journey are far-reaching. They extend beyond the confines of the healthcare system, touching upon broader questions of accountability, corporate responsibility, and the inherent value of human life. The quest for justice in the face of immense loss is a powerful testament to the human spirit, a relentless pursuit of truth and a commitment to ensuring that others do not suffer the same fate. Connie's memory serves as a constant reminder of this imperative, fueling my ongoing commitment to systemic reform and the pursuit of a more just and compassionate world. Her legacy is a call to action,

a demand for change that resonates far beyond the confines
of our personal tragedy. The fight continues. For Connie. For
all those who have suffered similar losses. For a better
future.

# The Human Cost of Negligence

The sterile, clinical environment of the hospital felt like a cruel mockery of the vibrant life Connie had led. The beeping monitors, the hushed whispers of nurses, the constant, pervasive scent of antiseptic – all served as a constant, jarring reminder of her absence. Her absence wasn't just a physical void; it was a gaping chasm in my life, in our life, that resonated with a pain so profound it threatened to consume me entirely. It wasn't just the grief, the agonizing, soul-wrenching grief; it was the injustice. The knowledge that her suffering, her premature death, could have been prevented.

The medical reports, initially a source of bewilderment and numb acceptance, later transformed into weapons in my fight for justice. Each line, each technical term, revealed a pattern of negligence, a series of missed opportunities, and ultimately, a disregard for human life in the pursuit of profit. The seemingly minor oversights – the delayed diagnosis, the misinterpretation of test results, the lack of timely intervention – coalesced into a devastating cascade of errors that cost Connie her life, leaving me stranded in a sea of sorrow, anger, and profound disillusionment.

The human cost of this negligence extended far beyond my personal grief. It shattered our family, leaving behind a void that could never be truly filled. Our children, already grappling with the unimaginable loss of their mother, were burdened by the additional weight of injustice. The image of their mother, vibrant, loving, and full of life, was now tainted by the memory of her suffering, the prolonged agony, and the feeling that her death was preventable. They watched me navigate the labyrinthine corridors of the legal system, witnessing my anger, my frustration, and my unrelenting pursuit of accountability. This fight, fueled by grief and a burning sense of justice, took its toll on them as well. The emotional strain, the anxieties, and the constant reminders of their loss created a ripple effect, shaping their lives in ways that remain palpable even now.

The financial burden added another layer of suffering. The medical expenses, the legal fees, the emotional toll—all exacted a heavy price on our family. We had always lived a life of comfortable means, but Connie's illness and subsequent death plunged us into a financial crisis, adding insult to injury. This wasn't just about money; it was about the resources that could have been used for her treatment, for her comfort, for creating precious memories in her final days. Those resources were lost, not only because of Connie's illness but also because of the failures of a system that prioritized profit over patient well-being. This financial strain intensified the emotional wounds, creating a sense of vulnerability and helplessness. The fight for justice became intertwined with a struggle for financial stability, a daunting task that added another dimension to our grief.

The emotional fallout reached far beyond our immediate family. Friends, colleagues, and members of our community were deeply affected by Connie's death. The shock, the disbelief, the shared grief – it was a collective trauma that bound us together in sorrow. Yet, alongside the collective grief, there was a shared sense of outrage. The people who knew Connie, who witnessed her kindness, her intelligence, her unwavering spirit, felt a visceral sense of injustice. Her loss resonated deeply with others, highlighting the vulnerability of individuals within a system designed to protect them. Their support provided an essential lifeline during this dark period, but their sorrow, their anger, served as a potent reminder of the far-reaching consequences of medical negligence.

Beyond the immediate impact on my family and friends, there was a growing awareness that Connie's case was not an isolated incident. It was a stark illustration of a larger problem, a systemic failure in the healthcare system that allowed for negligence and prioritized profit over patient care. I began to hear similar stories from others, heartbreaking accounts of avoidable deaths, missed diagnoses, and a pervasive culture of complacency within certain medical institutions. These narratives fueled my determination to fight for justice, not just for Connie, but for all those who had been victims of medical negligence. It became clear that this wasn't simply a matter of individual malpractice; it was a symptom of a deeper malaise, a corrosive system that tolerated, even encouraged, practices that prioritized profit over patient well-being.

The experience has profoundly altered my perspective on the nature of justice. It's not just about legal retribution; it's about systemic reform. It's about holding institutions accountable for their failures, about ensuring transparency and accountability within the healthcare industry, and about creating a system that truly prioritizes the well-being of patients. My pursuit of justice for Connie became a mission, a commitment to prevent similar tragedies from happening to others. This fight isn't just a personal crusade; it's a fight for systemic change, a fight to ensure that others do not suffer the same fate as my beloved Connie.

The legal battle was arduous, a protracted and emotionally draining process. The legal system, while designed to uphold justice, often seemed to amplify the pain, extending the grieving process and adding another layer of stress. The constant legal maneuvering, the depositions, the court appearances, all felt like an affront to Connie's memory. The initial outrage gradually gave way to a quiet determination, a resolve fueled by the memory of her life and a commitment to prevent similar tragedies.

Each legal victory, however small, felt like a testament to Connie's enduring spirit. Each obstacle overcome, each hurdle cleared, brought a sense of accomplishment, a small measure of solace amid the overwhelming grief. The legal battle was not simply about seeking financial compensation; it was about holding those responsible accountable for their negligence, and about bringing a measure of justice to a situation that felt profoundly unjust. It was about creating a public record of the failings, a testament to the cost of corporate negligence and the importance of patient safety. The fight itself, though emotionally draining, became a form of catharsis, a way of channeling the grief and anger into productive action.

The spiritual and philosophical lessons learned during this period have been profound. The experience forced me to confront the fragility of life, the transient nature of existence, and the enduring power of love. Connie's death, though devastating, also deepened my appreciation for the preciousness of life and the profound impact of human connection. The understanding that life is a gift, and a temporary one, heightened my awareness of the importance of living each day to its fullest.

The concept of karma, the belief that actions have consequences, has taken on new meaning. The negligence that contributed to Connie's death is not an abstract concept; it has real-world consequences, leaving a trail of destruction in its wake. The justice system, though imperfect, represents a mechanism for accountability, for acknowledging those consequences and striving to prevent similar actions in the future.

The search for meaning in the face of loss has led me to a deeper appreciation for the wisdom of figures like Lord Krishna and Chanakya. Their teachings on duty, dharma, and the importance of perseverance provided solace and guidance during this difficult period. The concept of dharma, of fulfilling one's duty, fueled my commitment to fighting for justice, not only for Connie but for others who have suffered similar losses. The wisdom of Chanakya, his strategic thinking, informed my approach to the legal battle, guiding me through the complexities of the system and helping me to navigate the challenges. Their teachings offered a framework for understanding the situation, providing guidance and hope amidst the despair.

The journey of grief and the pursuit of justice have been intertwined, inseparable strands of a complex tapestry. The pain of loss continues, a constant companion, but it is tempered by the conviction that Connie's life, her memory, her spirit, will not be forgotten. The fight continues, not just for personal closure but for broader systemic change. It's a fight for accountability, for transparency, and for a healthcare system that prioritizes patient well-being above all else. It's a fight to ensure that others do not suffer the same tragic loss that I have endured. It's a testament to the enduring power of love, the unwavering commitment to justice, and the unyielding spirit of a grieving husband determined to make a difference, honoring the memory of his beloved Connie. This is not merely a personal struggle; it is a fight for a better, safer, and more compassionate future.

## Advocating for Systemic Change

The sterile white walls of the hospital room, once a battleground against an unseen enemy, now stand as a chilling testament to a system's failures. Connie's absence echoes in the silence, a silence punctuated only by the phantom sounds of her breathing, the gentle rustle of her movements, the soft lilt of her laughter – memories that claw at my soul. The grief is a constant, a relentless companion, but it is no longer a solitary sorrow. It fuels a burning resolve, a righteous anger that pushes me to act, to fight, to ensure that no one else endures such a preventable loss. My personal tragedy has become a catalyst for a larger mission: advocating for systemic change within a healthcare system riddled with negligence and driven by profit over patient care.

This is not simply about seeking retribution; it's about demanding accountability. The initial shock of Connie's passing gradually gave way to a relentless questioning: were there missed opportunities? Was there a lack of vigilance? Were critical decisions clouded by factors that should have played no part in her treatment? The answers, gleaned through painstaking investigation and supported by expert medical opinions, painted a disturbing picture. A picture of a system where efficiency often supersedes empathy, where cost-cutting measures outweigh patient well-being, and where the pursuit of profit often overshadows the sacred duty of healing.

My fight began with the immediate – the pursuit of legal recourse against those whose negligence I believe contributed to Connie's death. This involved gathering medical records, consulting with legal experts, and preparing for a battle that felt as daunting as it was necessary. The legal process, however, is not merely a pursuit of justice for Connie; it is a strategic step toward achieving broader systemic reform. The legal challenge serves as a platform to expose the flaws, the loopholes, the insidious prioritization of profit over patient care that allowed Connie's suffering to become prolonged and ultimately, fatal.

The documentation unearthed during this legal process revealed a pattern of issues that extended far beyond Connie's individual case. I discovered instances of inadequate staffing, insufficient monitoring, delayed diagnosis, and a prevailing culture that prioritized speed and efficiency over careful consideration and personalized attention. These were not isolated incidents, but rather symptomatic of a much deeper malaise within the system. The legal battle, therefore, transformed from a personal crusade into a larger movement, a challenge not merely to an individual doctor or hospital but to the system itself.

But my advocacy extends far beyond the courtroom. I've discovered a community of individuals who have experienced similar tragedies, united by a shared grief and a shared determination to effect change. These stories – each heartbreaking in its uniqueness – reveal a systemic failure that transcends individual negligence. They reveal a pattern of preventable deaths, avoidable suffering, and a system desperately in need of reform. This shared experience has become a source of both strength and a renewed commitment to fight for a better healthcare system.

Sharing my story, initially a deeply personal act of mourning and seeking justice, has unexpectedly opened doors to collaborative efforts. I have engaged with patient advocacy groups, medical professionals who champion ethical practices, and legislators who understand the urgency of healthcare reform. Together, we are working to build a coalition dedicated to exposing negligence, advocating for transparency, and demanding better patient care. We are working to ensure that Connie's story, though unbearably painful, becomes a catalyst for change, preventing similar tragedies from occurring in the future.

Our collective work focuses on several key areas. First, we are advocating for stricter regulations regarding staffing levels and patient monitoring. The chronic understaffing in many medical facilities leads to overworked and stressed professionals, increasing the risk of errors and oversight. We need regulations that mandate safe staffing levels, ensuring that healthcare providers have the time and resources to provide the quality of care their patients deserve. This requires a significant investment in our healthcare system, a commitment that we believe is paramount. The lives saved, the suffering prevented, will far outweigh the cost.

Second, we are pushing for greater transparency in medical billing and hospital practices. The current system often obfuscates costs, making it difficult for patients and their families to understand the pricing structure and potential hidden fees. Increased transparency would empower patients to make informed decisions about their healthcare and hold institutions accountable for their practices. This level of openness is essential for fostering trust between patients and healthcare providers. The present lack of clarity breeds suspicion and makes it more difficult to hold negligent actors responsible for their actions.

Third, we are actively advocating for stronger regulations surrounding medical malpractice and improved reporting systems. The current system often allows negligent doctors and hospitals to operate with impunity. The process of filing malpractice claims is notoriously difficult and time-consuming, often discouraging victims from pursuing legal action. We need stricter regulations, simpler reporting procedures, and a commitment to holding negligent professionals accountable for their actions. This is not about creating a climate of fear, but about ensuring that those who make egregious errors are held responsible.

Fourth, we are working to promote a culture shift within the medical profession, emphasizing empathy and personalized care alongside technical expertise. The current focus on efficiency and productivity sometimes overshadows the fundamental human connection that is essential to patient care. A shift toward a more patient-centered approach, one that prioritizes the individual's needs and concerns, is crucial to improving the quality of care. This change will require a concerted effort on the part of medical schools, hospitals, and professional organizations to prioritize empathy and compassion in their training programs and workplace cultures.

Finally, our work focuses on educating the public about their rights as patients, empowering them to advocate for themselves and to seek justice when negligence occurs. Many patients are unaware of their rights or lack the resources to navigate the complex healthcare system. Through public awareness campaigns, educational materials, and support networks, we are empowering patients to become active participants in their own care and to demand accountability from healthcare providers. This level of empowerment is critical to fostering a system where patient well-being is truly paramount.

Connie's memory serves as a constant reminder of the devastating consequences of medical negligence. Her passing is not merely a personal tragedy; it is a wake-up call. It highlights the systemic issues within our healthcare system that need to be addressed urgently. The fight for justice is not just about seeking retribution; it's about creating a more just and equitable healthcare system, a system that prioritizes patient safety and well-being above profits. This is a fight worth fighting, a fight fueled by love, grief, and an unwavering commitment to ensuring that others do not suffer the same tragic loss that I have endured. It's a long road, but with each step, with each victory, however small, I honor Connie's memory and move closer to creating the systemic change we desperately need. The journey may be arduous, filled with setbacks and challenges, but the knowledge that I am working toward a better future, a safer future, sustains me. This is not about revenge; it is about redemption. It is about ensuring that Connie's life, and her death, become a force for positive change, a testament to the enduring power of love and the unwavering pursuit of justice. The fight for systemic change continues. It is a fight for Connie, for others, and for a future where the sanctity of life is truly valued above all else.

# Promoting Patient Safety

The sterile environment of the hospital, once a symbol of hope, now stands as a stark reminder of the fragility of life and the failures of a system designed to protect it. Connie's absence, a void that seems to swallow the very air around me, continues to fuel a fire within, a righteous anger tempered by a profound sorrow. The fight for justice is not merely a personal crusade; it's a fundamental commitment to patient safety, a principle that should be enshrined in the heart of every healthcare institution, not relegated to a footnote in a corporate balance sheet.

My professional background in crisis management has equipped me with the tools to analyze and dissect complex systems, to identify vulnerabilities and potential points of failure. The healthcare system, with its intricate web of protocols, regulations, and human interactions, is no exception. In Connie's case, the failure was not a singular event but a cascade of negligence, a systemic breakdown that allowed greed and apathy to supersede patient well-being. This is not about finger-pointing or assigning blame; it's about understanding the underlying mechanisms that allow such tragedies to occur, and implementing solutions to prevent them from happening again. It's about holding those responsible accountable, not for personal gratification, but to create systemic change.

The pursuit of justice demands a thorough understanding of the complexities of patient safety. This isn't merely about adhering to checklists and protocols; it's about fostering a culture of safety that permeates every level of the healthcare system. It starts with the fundamental recognition that patients are not commodities; they are individuals with unique needs and vulnerabilities. Their safety should be paramount, a guiding principle that trumps financial considerations or institutional convenience.

The medical establishment often operates within a framework of risk management, focusing on minimizing liability rather than maximizing patient safety. This approach is inherently flawed. It prioritizes avoiding legal repercussions over proactively preventing medical errors. A shift in paradigm is necessary; a culture of safety must replace the culture of liability. This necessitates a radical change in thinking, a fundamental realignment of values.

One critical aspect of improving patient safety is the implementation of robust reporting mechanisms. Medical errors must be treated not as shameful secrets to be hushed up, but as valuable learning opportunities to identify systemic weaknesses and prevent future incidents. A transparent and non-punitive system for reporting errors is crucial. Healthcare professionals should be encouraged, not discouraged, to report incidents, knowing that their reports will be used to improve patient safety rather than to incriminate them. A blame-free culture fosters open communication, allowing for a more thorough understanding of what went wrong and how it can be prevented.

Effective training and education play a crucial role in enhancing patient safety. Healthcare professionals at all levels must receive ongoing training on best practices, risk management, and the latest advancements in patient care. This should not be a one-time event but a continuous process of learning and development. Regular refresher courses and updates on protocols are essential to ensuring that healthcare professionals possess the skills and knowledge to provide safe and effective care. The development of standardized protocols and guidelines, implemented across all healthcare institutions, is also critical. This ensures consistency in care and helps minimize the risk of human error.

Technology also holds immense potential for improving patient safety. Electronic health records, for example, can reduce medication errors, improve communication between healthcare professionals, and enhance the overall quality of care. Furthermore, sophisticated monitoring systems can alert medical staff to potential problems in real-time, allowing for prompt intervention and preventing adverse events. Investment in technology, however, must be coupled with appropriate training and support to ensure that it is used effectively and efficiently.

Beyond technology and protocols, the human element remains critical. Effective communication between healthcare professionals, patients, and their families is paramount. Open and honest communication reduces misunderstandings, ensures that patients' concerns are addressed, and fosters trust. This also includes clear and concise explanations of medical procedures, treatment options, and potential risks. Patients should feel empowered to ask questions and participate actively in their care. A collaborative approach to healthcare fosters a sense of shared responsibility for patient safety. The patient is not a passive recipient of care; they are an active participant in their own well-being.

The ethical considerations surrounding patient safety are profound. The Hippocratic Oath's emphasis on "do no harm" underscores the fundamental responsibility of healthcare professionals to prioritize patient well-being. In a system driven by financial incentives, however, the ethical considerations can be overshadowed by profit motives. This imbalance must be addressed through stricter regulations, ethical guidelines, and increased oversight.

The pursuit of justice in healthcare is not solely about retribution; it's about achieving systemic change. It's about creating a healthcare system where patient safety is not merely a slogan but a foundational principle that guides every decision, every action, every interaction. Connie's memory, a constant source of both grief and inspiration, drives my commitment to this pursuit. Her absence is a gaping wound, but it is a wound that fuels a burning desire to prevent others from suffering a similar loss. The fight for patient safety is a fight for justice, for accountability, and for a healthcare system worthy of the trust it demands.

This is not just about regulations and protocols; it's about a fundamental shift in mindset. It's about recognizing that healthcare is a human endeavor, filled with inherent vulnerabilities, and that mitigating these vulnerabilities requires a constant commitment to learning, adapting, and improving. It necessitates a deep understanding of human factors – the psychology of error, the influence of fatigue, the impact of stress. It demands a healthcare system that values its professionals and equips them with the tools and support they need to provide safe, high-quality care. It involves fostering a culture of learning from mistakes, not punishing them. It necessitates a system designed to encourage transparency and accountability at all levels. And ultimately, it requires a renewed focus on the humanity of healthcare—recognizing that each patient is an individual with unique needs and vulnerabilities who deserves the utmost respect, care, and protection.

The journey toward a safer healthcare system is a long and arduous one, filled with challenges and setbacks. But the memory of Connie, the depth of my loss, and the unwavering commitment to justice continue to fuel my resolve. Each small victory, each step toward improvement, is a testament to the power of love, loss, and the enduring pursuit of a better future. It's a future where the greed and negligence that contributed to Connie's death are replaced by a culture of compassion, accountability, and a unwavering commitment to patient safety. It's a future where the sanctity of human life transcends the cold calculations of profit and loss. It is a future I will fight tirelessly to achieve, not just for Connie, but for all who deserve the highest standards of patient care. The fight continues, fueled by love, loss, and an unyielding belief in the power of justice.

# The Search for Meaning After Loss

The initial shock of Connie's absence was a physical blow, leaving me gasping for air in a world suddenly devoid of oxygen. It wasn't just the absence of her physical presence, the comforting weight of her hand in mine, the sound of her laughter echoing through our home. It was the absence of her mind, her spirit, the constant, vibrant dialogue that had defined our forty-one years together. Silence had replaced the symphony of our lives, a silence so profound it threatened to consume me entirely. The routines we'd meticulously built, the shared rituals, the unspoken understandings—all crumbled into dust, leaving me adrift in a sea of grief.

My experience in crisis management, a field demanding both emotional resilience and strategic thinking, proved strangely inadequate. I had managed crises for others, navigated the turbulent waters of organizational turmoil, offered solace and guidance to those caught in the undertow of loss. Yet, facing my own personal tsunami, I found myself grasping at straws, my carefully constructed coping mechanisms rendered useless. The tools I had used to help others felt clumsy and ineffective in my own hands. The grief was a raw, visceral experience, defying the logic and structure I relied upon.

The initial days blurred into a haze of emotional numbness, punctuated by moments of piercing pain that left me breathless. Sleep offered little respite, replaced by restless nights filled with vivid dreams, a constant replay of cherished memories intertwined with the agonizing reality of her absence. The world continued its relentless march forward, oblivious to the gaping hole in my life, a stark contrast to the stillness and sorrow that had become my constant companions. Every sunrise mocked my despair, each sunset a poignant reminder of the dwindling light in my own world.

The search for meaning began not with grand pronouncements or profound epiphanies, but with the small, almost imperceptible shifts in perspective. It started with the simple act of making coffee in the morning, a ritual we had shared for decades. The aroma, once a source of shared contentment, now brought a fresh wave of grief, but also a faint glimmer of recognition – life, in its everyday banality, persisted. It was in these mundane acts, in the repetitive gestures of daily living, that I began to rediscover a rhythm, a tentative structure amidst the chaos.

My crisis management background, however, did provide a crucial framework. It taught me the importance of structure, the need for a plan, even amidst overwhelming despair. I created a daily schedule, a simple routine that included walks in the park, meditation, and journaling. These actions, initially performed mechanically, slowly became anchors, offering a sense of control in a world that had become utterly unpredictable. The structure provided a sense of normalcy, a counterpoint to the turmoil within.

The pursuit of justice, my fight against the medical negligence I believed contributed to Connie's death, became another crucial element in my search for meaning. It was a way to channel my anger, to transform my despair into action. The process, though arduous and emotionally draining, offered a sense of purpose, a focus that helped pull me from the depths of my grief. It wasn't solely about retribution; it was about accountability, about preventing others from experiencing the same pain and loss. The fight for justice became a testament to Connie's memory, a way to honor her life by striving for a better world.

Lord Krishna's teachings, which Connie and I had often discussed, provided a different kind of solace. His emphasis on acceptance, on the transient nature of life and the inevitability of death, offered a framework for understanding my grief. It wasn't about denying the pain, but about accepting it as a part of the human experience, a necessary passage in the cycle of life and death. His teachings on dharma, on the importance of fulfilling one's duty, provided a sense of direction, a guiding principle for navigating the next phase of my life. It was not a passive acceptance of fate, but a proactive engagement with the challenges and opportunities that lay ahead.

Chanakya's wisdom, with its emphasis on pragmatism and strategic thinking, complemented Krishna's spiritual insights. Chanakya's teachings, rooted in the complexities of human nature and political realities, provided a practical counterpoint to the spiritual solace I found in Krishna's philosophy. It was through this synthesis of spiritual and philosophical perspectives that I began to piece together a new understanding of life, death, and my place in the world. It was a gradual process, a slow and often painful reconstruction of my identity and purpose.

The journey was not linear. There were setbacks, moments of intense grief that threatened to overwhelm me, periods of doubt and despair. But within those dark moments, there were also glimmers of hope, moments of unexpected joy, and the constant presence of Connie's memory, a guiding light that illuminated the path ahead. I learned to appreciate the small things, the simple pleasures that had once been taken for granted. A walk in the park, a cup of coffee, the warmth of the sun on my face—these mundane experiences became sources of comfort and gratitude.

The process of rebuilding my life involved redefining my goals and priorities. The ambitions and aspirations that had once driven me, once shared with Connie, now needed to be re-evaluated, reshaped to reflect my new reality. It was not a matter of abandoning my past, but of integrating it into a new narrative, a new chapter in the story of my life. This included re-establishing connections with friends and family, seeking support and understanding from those who loved Connie and me. It was a humbling experience, a recognition of my own vulnerability and the importance of human connection.

Giving back to the community became a way to channel my energy, to transform my grief into action. The fight for justice extended beyond my personal experience, becoming a broader advocacy for patient safety and healthcare reform. It was a way to honor Connie's memory while contributing to a larger cause. Volunteering at a local hospice offered a different kind of healing, allowing me to connect with others facing loss and providing support during their difficult times. The act of giving back, of helping others navigate their own journeys of grief, provided a profound sense of purpose and fulfillment.

The search for meaning after loss is not a destination, but an ongoing journey. It is a process of continuous growth, adaptation, and rediscovery. It is a path filled with both pain and joy, grief and gratitude. It is a testament to the enduring power of love, a reminder that even in the face of unimaginable loss, life continues, and within that continuation lies the opportunity for finding new meaning and purpose. The search for meaning is the journey of finding ourselves again, amidst the ashes of our past. The path is winding, but ultimately it leads to a stronger, wiser, and more compassionate self, ready to embrace the future, whatever it may hold. Connie's memory remains my constant companion, a source of strength, a reminder of the enduring power of love, a love that transcends even death.

## Redefining Life Goals and Priorities

The silence, once a deafening roar, had begun to soften, evolving into a melancholic hum. The sharp edges of my grief, though still present, had dulled slightly, polished smooth by the relentless passage of time. Yet, the void Connie left behind remained a gaping chasm in my life, a stark reminder of a love so profound it defied description. It was in this desolate landscape that I began to confront the daunting task of redefining my life, my goals, my very priorities. Forty-one years. Forty-one years of shared dreams, of meticulously crafted routines, of a life so intricately woven together that it felt impossible to unravel it without tearing the very fabric of my being. Now, the threads lay scattered, tangled, and broken.

The initial phase of my grief was dominated by a raw, visceral pain. It was a primal scream trapped in my throat, a relentless wave of sorrow that threatened to drown me. But as the intensity of that initial shock subsided, a different kind of pain emerged – a quieter, more insidious ache that settled deep within my bones. This was the pain of absence, the pain of realizing that the future I had envisioned, the future we had envisioned together, was irrevocably altered. It was a future where Connie's laughter didn't fill our home, where her hand wasn't intertwined with mine, where the quiet understanding that passed between us was silenced forever.

Rebuilding a life after such a profound loss felt like attempting to construct a magnificent cathedral using only rubble and shattered glass. Where did I begin? What did I even want to build? The carefully constructed edifice of our shared life had collapsed, leaving me with nothing but the debris of memories and the lingering scent of loss. The simple act of making coffee in the morning, once a shared ritual, now felt like an insurmountable task, a constant reminder of her absence.

My initial attempts at establishing a new routine were clumsy and forced. I tried to fill the emptiness with work, burying myself in my crisis management projects, hoping that the relentless demands of my profession would somehow numb the pain. But the work, once a source of satisfaction and fulfillment, now felt hollow, meaningless. It was a mere distraction, a temporary bandage on a deep and festering wound. The silence in my home was deafening, amplified by the empty chair across from my desk, a stark reminder of the woman who had been my constant companion, my confidante, my intellectual equal for more than four decades.

The pursuit of justice, my fierce determination to uncover the truth behind Connie's illness and the alleged medical negligence, became a singular focus. This wasn't simply a quest for retribution; it was a desperate attempt to find meaning in the face of unimaginable loss. It was an act of defiance, a refusal to accept the injustice of her premature death. The legal battles were grueling, draining every ounce of my energy, but they provided a sense of purpose, a tangible goal in the midst of overwhelming despair. Each step forward, each small victory, felt like a testament to Connie's memory, a validation of the life we had shared.

Yet, the legal battles, while providing a focus, were not a solution. They could not fill the void in my heart, nor could they bring Connie back. The truth was, I had to confront the reality of my new life, a life lived without her. This meant confronting not only the pain of her absence but also the profound shift in my personal priorities. What mattered now? What truly held value in this new reality?

The answers, when they came, were both unexpected and deeply personal. The intellectual pursuits that we had shared, once a source of shared joy, now became a form of solace. I delved deeper into philosophy, exploring the writings of Lord Krishna, Chanakya, and other spiritual thinkers, seeking answers to questions that had always lingered at the periphery of my awareness, but now felt urgent and vital. Their words, though written centuries ago, offered a surprising comfort, a sense of perspective and understanding. They reminded me of the cyclical nature of life and death, the impermanence of all things, and the importance of living each moment with intention and gratitude. These weren't just intellectual exercises; they were acts of spiritual survival.

Travel, another shared passion, became a form of pilgrimage. Visiting places we had dreamed of exploring together, I found myself connecting with Connie's memory in unexpected ways. The vibrant colors of a Tuscan sunset, the serenity of a Himalayan monastery, the bustling energy of a Moroccan souk – each location held echoes of her presence, her spirit, her love. These journeys weren't simply about sightseeing; they were about reconnecting with the world, about finding beauty and wonder amidst the pain.

My relationship with my family and friends also underwent a profound transformation. The support they offered, the simple acts of kindness and compassion, were invaluable lifelines in the stormy sea of my grief. I learned to rely on them, to accept their help, to allow myself to be vulnerable and dependent. This was a profound lesson, a humbling experience that taught me the importance of human connection and the power of community.

The art that Connie and I had cherished together now held a different significance. I found myself drawn to music, to painting, to sculpture – forms of expression that allowed me to process my emotions, to channel my grief into something tangible and meaningful. It was a form of creative therapy, a way of transforming pain into beauty.

The process of redefining my life goals and priorities wasn't a linear journey; it was a chaotic, often painful, and deeply personal exploration. It was a gradual shedding of old habits, old expectations, old versions of myself. It was a process of continuous adjustment, of trial and error, of constant growth and adaptation. It involved learning to accept the present moment, to embrace the uncertainty of the future, and to find gratitude in the midst of sorrow.

My new goals were not about achieving external success or accumulating material wealth. They were about cultivating inner peace, about deepening my understanding of the world and myself, about honoring Connie's memory in a way that was meaningful and authentic. My priorities shifted from the pursuit of ambition to the pursuit of meaning, from the accumulation of possessions to the cultivation of relationships, from the relentless pursuit of productivity to the embrace of stillness and reflection.

The void left by Connie's death will always be a part of me. It's a wound that will never fully heal, but it is a wound that I am learning to live with, to manage, to understand. The process of redefining my life after her death has been a journey of profound personal transformation. It has been a journey of grief, of healing, and of rediscovery. It has been a journey that has led me to a deeper appreciation for the fragility of life, the importance of love, and the enduring power of the human spirit. And it is a journey that continues, a journey that I will continue to walk, with Connie's memory as my guiding light. The search for meaning is not an ending, but a new beginning, a chance to build a life worthy of the love we shared, a life infused with purpose, gratitude and the quiet dignity of a love that transcends even death.

# Embracing New Opportunities

The unexpected death of my beloved Connie shattered my world, leaving me adrift in a sea of grief. The initial shock gave way to a profound and agonizing sorrow, a pain so raw and visceral that it threatened to consume me entirely. Yet, within the depths of this despair, a subtle shift began to occur. The relentless pressure of grief, while never fully subsiding, began to yield to a new kind of awareness. A space opened up, a space previously occupied by the overwhelming presence of my loss, now filled with the faintest glimmer of possibility. It wasn't a sudden blossoming of joy, but rather a quiet acceptance, a recognition that life, in its unpredictable cruelty, had also presented me with unforeseen opportunities.

One of the most significant shifts involved my perspective on time. Before Connie's illness, time was a commodity, something to be managed efficiently. Meetings, deadlines, appointments – these were the markers of my life. Now, time felt infinite and yet precious simultaneously. Each day was a gift, a fragile moment to be savored, a chance to honor Connie's memory not through melancholic remembrance, but through purposeful action. This new understanding led me to reassess my priorities. The relentless pursuit of professional success, once a defining characteristic of my life, felt trivial in comparison to the profound lessons learned through loss.

The legal battle, sparked by my belief in medical negligence contributing to Connie's death, consumed a significant portion of my energy in the months following her passing. Initially, driven by rage and a desperate need for justice, I poured myself into the legal process. The meticulous documentation, the countless meetings with lawyers, the grueling depositions – it became an almost obsessive pursuit. While the legal outcome was ultimately unsatisfying – a technicality preventing a full investigation – the process itself proved surprisingly cathartic. It forced me to confront my grief, to articulate my pain, and to channel my anger into constructive action. More than just a pursuit of justice, it became an act of honoring Connie's memory, a testament to our enduring bond.

In the wake of the legal proceedings, a different kind of opportunity emerged. The intense focus on the legal battle had inadvertently pushed aside other aspects of my life, particularly my creative endeavors. Connie and I had shared a deep love of the arts, frequently attending concerts, plays, and exhibitions. Her passing had left a gaping hole in this shared passion. However, the quiet moments after the legal battle offered an unexpected space for creative exploration. The pain, still present, now provided a fertile ground for self-expression. I began writing, initially as a means of processing my grief, of giving voice to the turbulent emotions that swirled within me. What began as a therapeutic exercise gradually evolved into a compelling narrative, ultimately transforming into this very book.

The act of writing became a pilgrimage, a journey of self-discovery fueled by the profound love I shared with Connie. Each word, each sentence, was a tribute to her, a testament to the depth of our connection. The process was not easy; there were moments of intense emotional pain, times when the memories were so vivid they threatened to overwhelm me. Yet, amidst the tears and the heartache, there was a sense of purpose, a feeling of honoring Connie's memory in a meaningful way. The writing became a bridge, connecting the past to the present, allowing me to navigate the complexities of grief while creating something beautiful from the ashes of loss.

Beyond the creative outlet, the journey through grief also led me to a deeper appreciation for the spiritual and philosophical concepts that had always been a part of my life. Connie and I shared a profound interest in Eastern philosophies, particularly the teachings of Lord Krishna and Chanakya. Their wisdom, previously appreciated intellectually, now resonated with a visceral depth. The concepts of dharma, karma, and the cyclical nature of life and death offered a framework for understanding Connie's passing, a lens through which to view my grief with a sense of acceptance and even serenity. This newfound perspective didn't erase the pain, but it shifted its intensity, transforming it from a destructive force into a catalyst for personal growth.

The grief, however, wasn't a solitary journey. The unwavering support of my friends and family proved invaluable, their presence a beacon of hope amidst the darkness. They didn't attempt to diminish my pain, nor did they offer facile solutions. Instead, they listened, they offered comfort, and they provided the space for me to grieve in my own way. Their understanding and empathy became a source of strength, reminding me that I wasn't alone in my struggle. This experience underlined the significance of human connection, the power of shared empathy, and the importance of allowing others to share in our burdens.

Another unexpected opportunity arose from the unexpected nature of Connie's death. Before her illness, our lives had been structured, predictable. We had established routines, plans, and expectations. Her death shattered that predictability, forcing me to confront the fragility of life. This understanding, however painful, led to a profound sense of freedom. I was no longer bound by the limitations of expectations, of pre-conceived notions of what my life "should" be. Instead, I was free to explore new possibilities, to pursue passions that had been previously sidelined, to redefine my identity beyond the role of husband.

This newfound freedom wasn't about abandoning the memories of Connie; instead, it was about integrating them into a broader narrative of my life. Her memory became a guiding principle, a source of inspiration for everything I undertake. It was a profound reminder of the importance of living a life filled with love, purpose, and a deep appreciation for the preciousness of each moment.

The process of redefining my life, of embracing these new opportunities, wasn't linear. There were days filled with intense sadness, moments of overwhelming grief that threatened to pull me under. But amidst these darker moments, there were also flashes of insight, moments of clarity, and the gradual emergence of a new sense of purpose. This purpose wasn't about replacing Connie or filling the void she left behind; it was about honoring her memory, by living a life worthy of the love we shared, a life infused with gratitude, and a quiet determination to make the most of the time I have remaining.

The journey continues, and I anticipate challenges and setbacks along the way. Yet, I approach the future with a renewed sense of hope, an understanding that grief, while profound and enduring, does not define the entirety of one's existence. It is a part of life, a difficult chapter, but not the final one. The lessons learned, the opportunities embraced, and the enduring power of love – these are the legacies of loss, the enduring gifts that have emerged from the profound sorrow of losing Connie. And these, I will carry with me always. They are not just my own, but a shared legacy, a testament to the enduring power of "Two Bodies & One

Soul." The loss is immense, but the love, the memory, and the lessons learned, those transcend even death. And that, in itself, is a powerful source of strength and a catalyst for building a future both meaningful and deeply personal. A future worthy of the love we shared, a future born from grief, forged in loss, but ultimately, shaped by hope.

## Giving Back to the Community

The quiet acceptance of my grief didn't magically erase the pain. Connie's absence remained a constant, a hollow space in my life that echoed with the memories of our shared laughter, our whispered secrets, the silent understanding that passed between us like a breath of air. But the pain, once a raging tempest, was now a persistent ache, a constant companion, but not my master. This shift, this subtle yet significant change, led me to a place of introspection, a place where I began to consider how to honor Connie's memory and find purpose amidst my loss. It wasn't about replacing her—that was an impossible task—but about finding a way to channel my grief, to transform its destructive energy into something positive, something that would resonate with her spirit and reflect the values we shared.

Connie and I had always believed in the importance of giving back to the community. We volunteered at local charities, supported numerous causes close to our hearts, and quietly offered assistance whenever and wherever we could. This wasn't a performative act; it stemmed from a deep-seated belief in the interconnectedness of humanity and a commitment to improving the lives of others. It was, in many ways, an extension of the love we shared – a love that extended beyond our personal lives to embrace the wider world. Now, in the wake of her passing, this belief became even more profound. It became a lifeline, a way to navigate the turbulent waters of my grief and, in a small way, to heal.

My initial efforts were tentative, almost hesitant. The sheer exhaustion of grief made even the smallest tasks feel monumental. But the support of friends, family, and even unexpected strangers helped me find the strength I didn't know I possessed. The outpouring of sympathy and compassion after Connie's death was overwhelming, a testament to the life she had lived and the impact she had made on those around her. It was in those expressions of love and support that I began to see a path forward, a way to channel my energy into something meaningful.

My first act was relatively small. I donated a significant portion of Connie's extensive art collection to the local museum, a collection she had lovingly curated over decades. It was a bittersweet experience, each painting, each sculpture, a vivid reminder of her passion, her talent, and our shared life. But in donating them, I felt a sense of purpose, a feeling that Connie's legacy would live on, her artistic spirit continuing to inspire others. The museum's curator, a kind and understanding woman, helped me through the process, understanding the emotional weight of the decision. Her empathy and support were invaluable during a time when I felt utterly lost.

The response to the donation was remarkable. The museum held a small exhibition in Connie's honor, featuring a selection of her best pieces. The opening was attended by friends, family, and members of the community, all drawn together by the shared memory of a talented and generous woman. Seeing her artwork displayed in such a prestigious setting, knowing that it would be enjoyed by others for years to come, brought a sense of comfort and peace. It was a tangible way to keep her spirit alive, a way to ensure that her creative energy would continue to inspire and uplift others. This was the first step in my journey of giving back, a journey that would lead me down unexpected and profoundly moving paths.

From there, my efforts expanded. I established a scholarship fund in Connie's name at her alma mater, providing financial assistance to promising art students who shared her passion and dedication. The application process itself was incredibly moving, reading the hopeful words of students who aspired to follow in Connie's footsteps, each application a testament to the power of art to transform lives. The selection committee, comprised of faculty members and art professionals, worked tirelessly to choose the recipients, their dedication echoing Connie's own commitment to excellence. Announcing the scholarship winners each year became a poignant ritual, a bittersweet reminder of Connie, but also a celebration of her enduring legacy.

Beyond the scholarship fund, I dedicated myself to supporting several charities that aligned with Connie's values. We had always been strong supporters of organizations dedicated to cancer research and care, and I continued this commitment, volunteering my time and contributing financially wherever possible. The work of these organizations, their tireless efforts to combat disease and provide comfort to those suffering, provided a powerful counterpoint to my grief. It was a way to focus my energy on something larger than myself, something that offered a sense of hope and purpose amidst the pain. The interaction with patients, families, and medical professionals provided a grounding reality, a reminder that despite the tragedy of loss, life continued, filled with both suffering and resilience.

I also became actively involved in advocating for improved patient care and medical transparency. Connie's death, though tragically caused by illness, was also complicated by what I believed to be medical negligence. This fueled a fire within me, a determination to seek justice and to prevent similar tragedies from happening to others. This was not simply a personal quest for retribution; it was a deeply ingrained sense of duty, a commitment to ensuring that other families would not have to endure the same pain and loss that I had experienced.

This advocacy work took many forms. I met with government officials, testified before legislative committees, and collaborated with patient advocacy groups to push for reforms in medical practices and transparency in hospital procedures. The process was often frustrating, the bureaucratic obstacles seemingly insurmountable. But the unwavering support of others, those who had experienced similar losses and those who shared my belief in the importance of justice, kept me going. Each small victory, each step forward, was a testament to the power of collective action and a reminder that even in the face of seemingly insurmountable odds, change is possible. It was a way to transform the destructive energy of my anger and frustration into something constructive, something that could make a tangible difference in the lives of others.

My journey of giving back wasn't confined to formal institutions or large-scale initiatives. It also encompassed simple acts of kindness, small gestures of compassion, and quiet moments of support offered to those in need. This included volunteering at a local soup kitchen, mentoring young people facing difficult circumstances, and simply offering a listening ear to those who needed it. These small acts, often unnoticed and unacknowledged, were deeply fulfilling, providing a sense of connection and purpose that went beyond the formal structures of charitable work. They were a reflection of Connie's own spirit of generosity and compassion, a testament to the enduring power of human kindness. The gratitude in the eyes of those I helped, their simple expressions of thankfulness, provided a solace that no amount of formal recognition could match.

Over time, this process of giving back became an integral part of my healing journey. It wasn't a cure for my grief—the pain of Connie's absence would always remain—but it transformed the way I experienced that pain. It provided a sense of purpose, a way to channel my energy into something constructive, and a way to honor Connie's memory and her legacy of compassion and service to others. In giving back to the community, I found a way to reconnect with the world, to find meaning and purpose amidst my loss, and to build a life worthy of the love we shared. It was a testament to the enduring power of "Two Bodies & One Soul," a testament to the love that transcended even death, and a testament to the enduring strength of the human spirit. The journey continues, always evolving, always learning, always giving. And in the giving, I find a kind of peace, a kind of healing, a kind of enduring connection to Connie, to life, and to the enduring beauty of the human spirit. The pain persists, but it no longer defines me. It is now but one thread in the rich tapestry of my existence, woven with the threads of love, loss, and the enduring power of hope.

## Living a Life of Purpose

The quiet acceptance of my grief didn't erase the void Connie left behind. Her absence remained a constant echo, a persistent ache in the fabric of my days. But the tempest had subsided, leaving a quieter, persistent pain. This subtle shift prompted deep introspection; I needed to honor Connie's memory, to find meaning and purpose in the wreckage of my loss. It wasn't about replacing her, an impossibility, but about transforming grief's destructive energy into something positive, something that resonated with her spirit and the values we cherished.

Our life together wasn't just about shared passions – travel, art, intellectual pursuits – it was about a commitment to making a difference. Connie's life was a testament to compassion and service. She volunteered tirelessly at the local hospice, finding solace in helping others navigate their own struggles. She believed in the power of giving, in the transformative potential of kindness, and she embodied those beliefs in every aspect of her life. Her spirit of service was deeply woven into the tapestry of our existence, and her passing left a gaping hole in the community as well as in my own heart.

This realization became my compass. I began to channel my grief into action, seeking ways to honor her legacy and, in doing so, honor the depth of our shared life. The legal battle against the medical negligence that contributed to Connie's suffering became a vital part of this process. It wasn't solely about retribution; it was about ensuring that others wouldn't suffer the same fate, a crusade born from the raw agony of loss, fueled by a deep sense of injustice.

Justice, however, is a complex and often elusive concept. The legal system, while designed to provide redress, often falls short of providing true closure. My efforts, though ultimately successful in achieving some accountability, left me pondering the limitations of legal justice. The pain persisted, but it transformed. It was no longer simply a consuming anguish, it was a potent fuel, driving my desire to create lasting positive change.

Beyond the legal fight, I found purpose in reconnecting with my community. I joined the board of the local hospice where Connie had volunteered, immersing myself in the work she loved. It was a way to be closer to her spirit, a way to surround myself with the values she cherished. The work was challenging, at times deeply emotional, but it filled a void within me. The faces of the patients and their families, the shared struggles and quiet triumphs, reminded me of the profound beauty of human connection, of the strength of the human spirit in the face of adversity. And, in serving others, I found a way to serve Connie's memory, to keep her spirit alive in the world.

This involved more than simply volunteering my time. I channeled my experiences into writing, drawing upon my background in crisis management and my deep understanding of spiritual and philosophical concepts. My book, "Two Bodies & One Soul," became a powerful outlet for my grief, a way to process my pain and share Connie's story with the world. It was a testament to our love, a celebration of our life together, and a testament to the enduring power of the human spirit. Writing the book wasn't just a therapeutic process, but a purposeful undertaking, a way to contribute to the broader conversation about loss, grief, and the search for meaning.

The act of writing itself became a kind of meditation. As I poured my heart onto the page, I found a sense of clarity, a way to navigate the labyrinth of my emotions. The words themselves became a form of therapy, a way to express the inexpressible, to articulate the depth of my love and loss. The process demanded honesty, vulnerability, and a willingness to confront my deepest fears and insecurities. But in the act of sharing my story, I discovered a sense of peace, a sense of purpose, and a profound connection to my late wife's memory. This writing project far exceeded my expectations, allowing for healing and the opportunity to give back to the community through sharing the experiences and knowledge gained in life.

Moreover, my commitment to living a life of purpose extended beyond the individual sphere. I began to explore ways to address the systemic issues that had contributed to Connie's suffering. I became actively involved in advocacy for better medical care, working to improve the quality of healthcare for others. This was a natural extension of my legal fight, a way to amplify my voice and advocate for change on a larger scale. The experiences of the previous year and the years that passed since Connie's death had transformed my grief into a catalyst for positive change.

This advocacy work drew on my experiences in crisis management, providing me with a unique perspective and a skillset that was valuable in navigating the complex world of healthcare reform. I worked closely with policymakers, healthcare professionals, and patient advocacy groups to implement meaningful changes. It was a challenging and often frustrating undertaking, but the sense of purpose fueled my determination to persevere. It was a tangible way to honor Connie's memory, to ensure that her suffering didn't go in vain, and to help prevent similar tragedies from happening to others. This advocacy became a powerful source of healing, transforming the pain of loss into a force for positive change.

The journey wasn't always easy. There were days when the weight of my grief felt overwhelming, days when the pain felt too profound to bear. But the commitment to living a life of purpose provided a lifeline, a way to navigate the darkness and find glimmers of hope. The combination of creative writing and advocacy work provided a path towards healing and a sense of purpose. The act of giving back, of contributing to the world in a meaningful way, filled the void that Connie's absence had created.

My understanding of spiritual and philosophical concepts—drawing upon the wisdom of Lord Krishna, Chanakya, and others—offered guidance and perspective during times of intense struggle. The teachings of these figures emphasized the importance of selfless action, of living a life dedicated to the greater good, and of finding peace amidst suffering. These concepts offered a framework for understanding my loss, for finding meaning in my pain, and for transforming my grief into a force for positive change. The spiritual path became a beacon of hope, guiding me through the darkness and toward a future built on purpose and gratitude. It underscored the interconnectedness of all beings, reminding me that my actions had ripple effects, extending far beyond my own personal experience.

In the years since Connie's passing, I've come to understand that grief is not a linear process. It's a journey, a winding path that leads through unexpected twists and turns. There are moments of profound sadness, moments of intense longing, and moments of unexpected joy. But amidst the chaos and uncertainty, the commitment to living a life of purpose has provided a constant anchor, a way to navigate the complexities of grief and find meaning in the face of loss. This journey is a testament to the strength of the human spirit and the profound power of love, a love that transcends even death itself. The enduring legacy of Connie and my shared experiences continue to shape my life, guiding my actions and fueling my commitment to serve others. And in that service, I find a profound and lasting connection to the woman I loved, to the life we shared, and to the enduring power of the human spirit. The pain remains, a constant reminder of her absence, but it no longer defines me. It is now woven into the tapestry of my existence, a testament to the depth of our love and the enduring power of hope.

# A Lasting Legacy of Love

Forty-one years. A lifetime woven together, thread by painstaking thread, into a tapestry so rich, so vibrant, so uniquely *ours* , that even the cruel shears of death cannot entirely unravel it. Connie's absence is a wound that bleeds perpetually, a constant ache that reminds me of the irreplaceable void she left behind. Yet, within that aching void, a different kind of strength blossoms, a strength forged in the crucible of grief, tempered by the unwavering memory of our love. This is not a resignation to loss, but a defiant affirmation of the life we shared, a testament to the enduring power of a bond that transcends the physical realm.

It wasn't just a marriage; it was a partnership, a shared journey of discovery, a dance of two souls intertwined. We built a life together, brick by painstaking brick, a life rooted in mutual respect, shared passions, and an unwavering commitment to each other's growth. From the bustling streets of our early years to the quiet comfort of our later decades, our love was the constant, the unwavering north star guiding us through every storm. We navigated life's complexities together, celebrating triumphs and weathering setbacks with a resilience that only deepened our connection. Our love wasn't a passive sentiment; it was an active force, a shaping power that molded our individual selves into something greater, something more profound.

The memories flood back – a kaleidoscope of shared moments, each one a jewel reflecting the multifaceted brilliance of our love. The exhilaration of our first trip to the Himalayas, the shared awe at the breathtaking beauty of the landscape, the quiet intimacy of our evenings spent under a star-studded sky. The thrill of discovering a hidden gem in a dusty antique shop in Florence, the shared laughter as we navigated the chaotic streets of Marrakech, the quiet satisfaction of completing a challenging jigsaw puzzle together on a rainy afternoon. Each memory is a precious fragment, a piece of the puzzle that was our life together, and piecing them together now, in the quiet solitude of my grief, allows me to reconstruct, to relive, to cherish the totality of what we shared.

It wasn't just the grand adventures, the exotic travels, the intellectual pursuits that defined our bond. It was the smaller moments, the seemingly insignificant details, the quiet gestures of affection, the shared silences filled with unspoken understanding, the comfortable rhythm of our daily routines that truly embodied the depth of our connection. It was in the simplest acts – a cup of tea shared in the morning, a hand held across a crowded room, a shared glance across a table – that the profoundest expressions of our love resided. These memories aren't just pleasant recollections; they are potent reminders of the richness and depth of our shared life, a life that continues to resonate even in the face of death.

The pain of her absence is still raw, a wound that time hasn't yet fully healed. I still find myself reaching for her hand, searching for her presence, longing for her laughter. The quiet corners of our house echo with her absence, a void that no amount of time or effort can completely fill. Yet, within this pain, within this profound loss, I find a different kind of strength, a resilience that comes from the very depth of my grief. It's a strength that reminds me of Connie's own unwavering spirit, her resilience in the face of her illness, her determination to live life to the fullest, even as death loomed.

This book, this journey through grief and memory, hasn't been an easy process. The writing itself became a form of therapy, a way to process the overwhelming emotions, to confront the anger and frustration that still linger, to celebrate the profound love that was, and in a way, still is, the defining force of my life. It's a way to honor Connie's memory, not just by remembering her, but by sharing the essence of who she was with the world. To ensure that her legacy, her spirit, continues to live on in the hearts and minds of others.

The anger I felt, and still feel, regarding the potential medical negligence that contributed to Connie's suffering and death, remains a powerful motivator. It wasn't just about seeking justice for Connie; it was about ensuring that others don't suffer the same fate. It was about shining a light on the systemic issues within the healthcare system, the greed and negligence that can have such devastating consequences. My background in crisis management equipped me with a certain fortitude and determination. The fight for accountability was not merely a legal battle; it was a moral imperative, a fight for justice and a commitment to preventing similar tragedies from happening to others. The pursuit of justice wasn't about retribution; it was about creating a system where patients are truly valued, where their well-being is prioritized, where negligence is met with accountability.

The teachings of Lord Krishna and Chanakya, which I delved into during Connie's illness and after her passing, proved invaluable in navigating the tumultuous waters of grief. Krishna's emphasis on acceptance, on finding peace amidst suffering, provided a framework for understanding my pain. Chanakya's wisdom, with its focus on duty, justice, and navigating life's complexities, fueled my determination to fight for accountability and to find meaning in my loss.

The integration of these spiritual and philosophical perspectives helped me find a path forward, a way to channel my grief into something productive, something meaningful.

Rebuilding my life after Connie's death has been a gradual, often painful process. It's been about rediscovering myself, redefining my purpose, and finding new ways to experience joy and fulfillment. It's about embracing self-care, nurturing my emotional and physical well-being, and rebuilding the support systems that help me navigate the challenges of life. It has also involved embracing new opportunities, new experiences, and seeking new connections. It is a continuous process, a journey with ups and downs, but a journey filled with hope and purpose.

Connie's legacy is not merely a collection of memories; it's a living testament to the power of love, a beacon illuminating the path forward for others grappling with loss. Her spirit lives on in the ripple effects of her kindness, her dedication, and the profound love she shared with everyone who knew her. Her laughter still echoes in my heart, a melody that time cannot erase. Her wisdom, her strength, her unwavering spirit continue to inspire me, to guide me, to sustain me.

And so, I continue. I live not in spite of Connie's absence, but because of the indelible mark she left on my life. Her love is a constant companion, a source of strength and inspiration, a reminder that even in the face of unimaginable loss, love endures. It transcends death, it transcends time, it transcends the limitations of the physical world. This is the legacy of Connie, the enduring power of a love that was, is, and always will be, two bodies, one soul, forever. And that is a legacy I will carry with me, always. This is not just a story of loss; it's a story of enduring love, a testament to the resilience of the human spirit, and a beacon of hope for all those who grieve. It is a testament to the power of love that transcends even death itself.

# The Power of Memory

The scent of her perfume, a subtle blend of jasmine and sandalwood, still lingers faintly in the air, a phantom echo of her presence. It's a cruel and beautiful torment, this lingering memory, a constant reminder of what I've lost, yet also a lifeline to the life we shared. It's in these sensory memories, these fragments of the past, that Connie remains vibrantly alive for me. The rustle of her silk scarf as she turned to greet me, the warmth of her hand in mine during our evening strolls, the cadence of her laughter, a melody that still plays in the chambers of my heart – these are not just recollections; they are the building blocks of an enduring love, a testament to a life lived fully and passionately. They are the sustenance that keeps my spirit alive, a defiant act against the encroaching despair of grief.

This is the power of memory. It's not merely the act of recalling events; it's the active preservation of love, the conscious choice to keep the flame of our shared history burning brightly. It's a conscious defiance of oblivion. Each memory, a precious jewel, meticulously preserved within the vaults of my mind, carefully dusted and polished, forever held close to my heart. It's a deliberate act of love, a testament to the enduring strength of our bond. It's in the remembering, in the reliving, in the re-experiencing of these shared moments, that Connie continues to live. She is not just a ghost of the past, a faded photograph in an old album; she is a vibrant presence, a constant companion, a love that transcends the confines of mortality.

This conscious act of remembering isn't passive; it's a labor of love, a sacred duty I've undertaken to honor her memory. I meticulously curate these memories, revisiting our old photographs, rereading our letters, listening to our favorite music. I actively seek out reminders of her—a particular shade of blue that reminded me of her eyes, the fragrance of the lilies she adored, the taste of her favorite chai. Each encounter brings a surge of bittersweet emotion, a mixture of overwhelming sorrow and deep affection. But within this sorrow, a profound peace resides. This peace is not a surrender to grief, but a conscious choice to embrace the love we shared, to live in harmony with the bittersweet reality of our loss. It is a testament to Connie's enduring influence on my life, a constant reminder of the life we shared and the values we embraced together.

Our shared life wasn't just a collection of events; it was a narrative woven with shared dreams, ambitions, and disappointments. We travelled extensively, immersing ourselves in the vibrant cultures of Asia, the serene landscapes of Europe, the bustling cities of North America. Each trip, a chapter in our story, filled with shared experiences, laughter, and moments of profound connection. I recall the hushed reverence we felt standing before the Taj Mahal, the breathtaking beauty of the Amalfi Coast, the vibrant energy of the Marrakech souks. These were not just tourist experiences; they were moments of shared intimacy, profound connection, shared discovery. They were moments of a lifetime, now deeply etched in my memory. These are not just tourist snapshots; they are deeply personal experiences, each one a memory that I return to often, not only to remember the places, but to feel Connie's presence once more.

Our shared intellectual pursuits are another wellspring of precious memories. The hours spent discussing philosophy, delving into the intricacies of history, debating the merits of different artistic movements – these were the cornerstones of our intellectual life, a rich tapestry of shared interests and intellectual exploration. We spent countless evenings discussing the profound wisdom of Lord Krishna's Bhagavad Gita, the shrewd strategies of Chanakya, the poetic insights of Rumi. These conversations weren't mere intellectual exercises; they were bonding moments that deepened our understanding of ourselves and the world around us, shaping our values and our perspectives. I revisit these intellectual discussions often, engaging with the texts we studied together, feeling her presence in the silent contemplation, her voice echoing in my thoughts.

Even the moments of conflict, the disagreements, the inevitable friction that arose in any long-term relationship, are now precious memories, albeit tinged with a bittersweet undertone. These weren't moments of estrangement but rather opportunities for growth, for understanding, for deepening our connection. They were opportunities to learn from each other, to forge a stronger, more enduring bond, a testament to the resilience of our relationship. Recalling these conflicts, I understand that even the disagreements strengthened our love, refining it, and making it more profound.

The pain of her illness, the harrowing ordeal of her treatment, the agonizing final weeks, these memories are the most difficult to bear. Yet, they are also a testament to the depth of our love, to the unwavering support we provided each other, to the strength and resilience we found within ourselves. It was during these difficult times that our bond deepened, our love becoming an unbreakable shield against despair. Remembering these harrowing experiences allows me to acknowledge the profound pain I experienced, to process the feelings of anger and injustice stemming from perceived medical negligence. This process, while agonizing, is necessary for healing, for acceptance.

But beyond the pain, the memories of those final days remain a source of profound peace. The unwavering love, the unspoken promises, the silent strength – these intangible elements of our final moments are woven into the fabric of my memory, a reminder of the enduring power of love in the face of death. These experiences, though painful, were also some of the most intimate and profound moments of our relationship, a testament to the love that transcended the physical world.

My quest for justice, the relentless pursuit to expose the alleged medical negligence that contributed to Connie's untimely death, is fueled by a desire to honor her memory, to prevent others from suffering the same anguish. It's a mission undertaken not out of vengeance but out of a deep-seated sense of justice, a fierce commitment to ensuring that no one else experiences such a preventable tragedy. This pursuit, driven by grief, is an integral part of my healing process, my tribute to Connie. The fight for justice, born from sorrow, becomes a meaningful act of love in her memory.

The memories of Connie are not just a collection of past events; they are the essence of my being. They are the foundation upon which I rebuild my life, the compass that guides my journey forward. They are not just recollections; they are the very fabric of my existence. They are my anchor, my solace, my strength. They are a testament to the profound and enduring nature of love, a love that transcends time, space, and even death itself. This is the legacy of Connie, a testament to the enduring power of a love that was, is, and always will be, two bodies, one soul, forever. And this is a legacy I will cherish, and carry forward, forever.

## Hope for the Future

The scent of jasmine and sandalwood, a ghost of Connie's perfume, still clings to my memory, a bittersweet reminder of our shared life. Grief, like a relentless tide, continues to ebb and flow, sometimes a gentle lapping at the shore of my consciousness, other times a crashing wave that threatens to engulf me. Yet, even in the darkest depths of sorrow, a flicker of hope persists, a fragile flame in the storm. It's not a naive optimism that denies the pain, but rather a quiet acceptance of life's paradoxical nature – a tapestry woven with threads of joy and sorrow, light and shadow. Connie's absence is a constant ache, a void that will never be completely filled, but it is not a void that defines me. It is a space that allows for the growth of something new, a space for the cultivation of resilience, understanding, and a deeper appreciation for the fleeting beauty of life. It is a space where I can honor her memory not through paralyzing grief, but through purposeful living.

This hope doesn't negate the raw, visceral pain I still feel. There are days when the weight of loss feels unbearable, when the silence in the house screams louder than any sound ever could. I find solace in quiet moments, in the simple act of tending to our garden, a space we cultivated together, a sanctuary where memories blossom alongside the roses and lilies she loved. Each bloom, each carefully nurtured plant, is a tangible reminder of her presence, a testament to the life we built together, a life that continues to resonate within me. The garden, much like my memories of Connie, is a vibrant testament to our shared journey, a living memorial that both celebrates her life and acknowledges the enduring pain of her absence.

My journey through grief has been a profound exploration of self, forcing me to confront not only the pain of loss, but also the unexamined aspects of my own being. The process of writing this book itself has been a form of catharsis, a way of ordering the chaos of my emotions, of giving voice to the silent screams echoing in the emptiness left behind. It has allowed me to process my anger, my frustration with the perceived negligence that may have contributed to Connie's suffering, and to find a measure of peace in the act of storytelling. The legal battles, though draining and emotionally taxing, have become a symbol of my commitment to ensuring that no one else experiences the same injustice we faced. Seeking justice for Connie has become a vital part of my healing process; it's a way to honor her memory, not through vengeance, but through advocacy for change and better care. The pursuit of justice, therefore, is not simply a legal pursuit but a deeply personal one, a continuation of our shared values. It's a testament to the unwavering belief we both had in a just and equitable world.

This quest for justice has, paradoxically, led me to a deeper understanding of forgiveness. It is not about condoning negligence or absolving those responsible for Connie's suffering, but about releasing the corrosive power of resentment from my own heart. It's a journey of letting go, of accepting that I cannot change the past, but that I can shape my future. Forgiveness, in this context, is not a weakening, but an act of self-liberation, allowing me to move forward without being shackled by the weight of bitterness. The path to forgiveness is a long and arduous one, but it is an essential part of finding healing and peace in the aftermath of loss.

Beyond the legal battles and the personal struggles, I find solace in the enduring power of our shared values. Connie and I shared a deep love for learning, for intellectual discourse, for the beauty of nature and art. These passions, nurtured over four decades, are not extinguished by her death. Instead, they serve as guiding lights, illuminating the path forward. They are the anchors that keep me tethered to a sense of purpose, a sense of meaning, even in the face of profound loss. Continuing to pursue our shared passions, to read, to learn, to travel (though it feels different now), to explore the world's artistic wonders – these are not just personal pursuits, but ways of keeping Connie's spirit alive within me. They are ways of honoring her legacy, celebrating her life and its impact.

Moreover, my understanding of spiritual and philosophical concepts, long shared with Connie, provides a framework for understanding loss and navigating grief. The wisdom of figures like Lord Krishna, whose teachings emphasize the impermanence of life and the importance of selfless action, and Chanakya, whose astute political observations highlighted the importance of justice and fairness, continue to guide me. Their wisdom resonates even more profoundly now, lending a sense of perspective and a grounding force in the midst of the emotional turmoil. Their teachings provide both context for understanding the complexities of life and loss and a roadmap for forging a meaningful path forward. These teachings, so deeply intertwined with our lives and discussions, offer a profound sense of comfort and direction during this difficult time.

The future remains unwritten, a vast and uncertain landscape. There are moments of intense loneliness, a profound sense of emptiness that threatens to consume me. Yet, within that emptiness, there is also the possibility for growth, for rediscovery, for the forging of new connections and the cultivation of new passions. I do not envision a future where Connie's memory fades or her love diminishes. Her presence continues to shape my thoughts, actions, and hopes for the future. It is a presence that inspires me to live with purpose, to honor her legacy through my actions, and to strive to create a world that is more just, more compassionate, and more loving.

Perhaps the most profound realization is that Connie's death has not diminished our love; it has transformed it. It is no longer a love lived in the tangible world of shared moments and physical intimacy, but a love that transcends the boundaries of death, a love that resides in my heart, in my memories, in every aspect of my being. It's a love that continues to guide and sustain me, a love that fuels my determination to fight for justice, and a love that inspires me to live a life worthy of the legacy we built together.

My hope for the future is not an expectation of happiness free from sorrow but a quiet acceptance of life's complexities, an understanding that grief and joy, pain and peace, can coexist. It's a hope rooted in the enduring power of love, a love that transcends the limitations of time and space. It's a hope that allows me to carry Connie's memory, not as a burden, but as a source of strength and inspiration, guiding me on a path of purpose, healing, and continued love. It is a hope that reminds me that even in the face of profound loss, life continues, a testament to the enduring spirit of love and the possibilities that lie ahead. It is a hope that allows me to believe that, somehow, somewhere, our two souls remain connected, eternally bound by a love that knows no end.

The journey ahead will be challenging, filled with moments of profound sadness and unexpected joy. But the memories we created, the love we shared, the values we cherished – these are the cornerstones upon which I rebuild my life, the foundation upon which I find strength and hope. They are the testament to a life lived fully and passionately, a life that transcends the boundaries of death, a life that remains vibrantly alive in my heart. And it is within these memories, these shared experiences, that I find not only the strength to carry on, but also the profound hope for a future worthy of the love we shared – a future where Connie's spirit continues to live on, not just in my heart, but in the world around me. The journey continues, a journey of healing, a journey of remembrance, a journey of love that transcends time and death – two bodies, one soul, forever.

# A Message of Resilience

The quiet hum of the morning light filtering through the windowpanes is a constant companion now, a gentle reminder of the passage of time. Time, that relentless river, continues its inexorable flow, carrying with it the echoes of laughter, the weight of sorrow, and the subtle shift of seasons. Connie is gone, her physical presence a cherished memory, yet her essence, her spirit, remains interwoven with the fabric of my being. It's a feeling both profound and strangely comforting, a testament to the enduring power of love that transcends the limitations of mortality.

This isn't a simple platitude, a convenient balm for a wounded soul. It is a hard-won truth, forged in the crucible of grief, tempered by the relentless passage of days, weeks, months, and years since her passing. The initial shock, the raw, visceral pain of loss, has slowly given way to a more nuanced understanding, a quiet acceptance of life's inherent fragility and the immutable reality of death. Yet, this acceptance is not resignation; it is not a surrender to despair. Rather, it is the foundation upon which resilience is built.

The fight for justice, the relentless pursuit of accountability for the alleged medical negligence that contributed to Connie's untimely death, continues. This battle, while deeply personal, also carries a broader significance. It is a fight for integrity, for ethical practice in the medical profession, for a system that values human life above profit and expediency. It's a fight I wage not only for Connie, but for all those who have suffered similar losses, those who have been victims of negligence and indifference. The legal battles are long and arduous, filled with complexities and delays, but the pursuit of justice itself, the unwavering commitment to truth, fuels a vital part of my healing process. It gives a focus to my grief, channeling the raw pain into a purposeful act.

My grief is not a monolith; it is a multifaceted experience, a kaleidoscope of emotions that shift and change with the ebb and flow of time. There are days when the sun shines brightly, and I find myself enveloped in a wave of cherished memories—our travels through the Tuscan countryside, our laughter echoing through the Louvre, the shared thrill of discovering a rare first edition. These moments are precious gifts, fleeting glimpses of a joy that persists even in the face of loss. Then there are days when the shadows loom large, when the weight of absence is almost unbearable. These are the days I lean on the support of friends, family, and the wisdom I've gleaned from years of study and reflection. The teachings of Lord Krishna, the strategic insights of Chanakya, the comforting embrace of spiritual practices – these are not mere intellectual pursuits but life rafts in the storm. They provide a framework for understanding, a path toward acceptance, and a source of enduring strength.

The concept of "two bodies, one soul" is not merely a romantic notion; it is a reflection of the profound interconnectedness that Connie and I shared. Our lives were intertwined, our dreams and aspirations woven together like threads in a rich tapestry. Even now, separated by the veil of death, I feel her presence, her influence, guiding my steps, shaping my choices. This is not a hallucination or delusion; it is the enduring power of love, the legacy of a life lived fully and passionately. The love we shared resonates not just within my heart, but in the very air I breathe, in the quiet spaces between my thoughts.

Resilience is not the absence of pain; it is the capacity to navigate the complexities of grief, to find meaning and purpose amidst sorrow. It is the courage to confront the challenges that life inevitably throws our way, to rise above adversity, and to embrace the opportunities for growth and transformation that emerge from even the darkest of experiences. It is the ability to nurture the flame of hope, even when the winds of despair blow fiercely.

The journey toward healing is not a linear progression; it is a winding path, filled with unexpected turns and detours. There are moments of breakthrough, where clarity emerges from the fog of grief, and there are moments of relapse, when the pain seems almost unbearable. It is essential to allow oneself to feel the full spectrum of emotions, to honor the pain without being consumed by it. To weep when necessary, to rage against the injustice of loss, and to celebrate the joy of memories. Suppression of emotions only prolongs the healing process. It is through the acceptance of the full human experience—the joys and sorrows, the triumphs and setbacks—that we find true resilience.

Connie's absence is a profound void, but it is not a void that defines me. It is a space for growth, a catalyst for transformation. In her memory, I strive to live a life worthy of the love we shared—a life of purpose, of compassion, of unwavering commitment to justice. I find strength in the knowledge that her spirit continues to live on, not only in my heart, but in the ripple effect of her influence on the world. She instilled in me the importance of integrity, of pursuing truth relentlessly, and of never giving up on hope.

My experience isn't unique; millions grapple with similar losses, battling grief, searching for meaning, seeking justice. The lessons I have learned, the wisdom I have gained, are not solely for my benefit. They are intended to resonate with others who share this profound experience. The message of resilience, of hope amidst despair, is a message of universality. It is a testament to the human spirit's capacity to endure, to adapt, and to find beauty even in the face of profound loss. The journey continues, a journey of healing, a journey of remembrance, a journey of love that transcends the boundaries of time and death. It's a journey I undertake with the unwavering conviction that the love we shared, the life we built together, will continue to resonate far beyond the confines of our earthly existence. And in that shared love, in that enduring connection, lies the profound and enduring power of resilience. The strength to carry on, to live, to love, to fight for justice, to honour her memory - not through paralyzing grief, but through purposeful living - is the greatest tribute I can offer. The jasmine and sandalwood still linger; but now, they're interwoven with the fragrant bloom of resilience, a testament to the enduring power of love that even death cannot erase.

The legal battles continue, but the focus has subtly shifted. It's less about personal retribution and more about systemic change. I'm using my experience, my expertise in crisis management, to advocate for improvements in medical protocols, patient safety, and accountability. Connie's memory fuels my advocacy, transforming my grief into a catalyst for positive change. I'm working with patient advocacy groups, contributing to policy discussions, and sharing my story to help others avoid the pain we endured. This new purpose is profoundly healing. It's a way to honor Connie's legacy, to ensure that her suffering wasn't in vain.

The philosophical and spiritual reflections remain crucial. They provide a framework for understanding the complexities of life and death, offering solace and guidance in times of intense emotional turmoil. The teachings of Lord Krishna on dharma and karma offer a perspective on the larger cosmic order, placing individual experiences within a broader context. Chanakya's pragmatism helps me navigate the practical challenges of rebuilding my life, focusing on concrete steps rather than being overwhelmed by the enormity of my loss. This blend of pragmatism and spirituality is vital for navigating the unpredictable journey of grief. It offers a solid foundation for building a new life, a life infused with meaning and purpose.

The memories we shared, the laughter, the adventures, the quiet moments of shared intimacy—these are more than just reminiscences; they are the building blocks of my new reality. They are the anchors that keep me grounded during turbulent times. I revisit them often, not to dwell on the past, but to draw strength and inspiration from the love we shared. These memories serve as a constant reminder of the extraordinary life we lived together, a life filled with passion, purpose, and unwavering love. The void Connie's absence has created is slowly filling with new experiences, new relationships, new pursuits—but it's a space infused with the spirit of who she was and the life we shared. It's a testament to the enduring nature of love, its capacity to transcend even the finality of death.

The resilience I've discovered is not a static state; it's a dynamic process, a continuous evolution. It's a testament to the human spirit's incredible capacity to adapt, to heal, and to find meaning even in the face of unimaginable loss. It's not about forgetting Connie; it's about remembering her in a way that celebrates her life, honors her legacy, and empowers me to live a life that is both meaningful and purposeful. It's a life that embraces the full spectrum of human emotion, accepting the joy alongside the sorrow, the light alongside the shadow. The journey continues, ever evolving, ever deepening, ever more profoundly shaped by the love that transcends time and death. Two bodies, one soul, forever. That remains the enduring truth, the unwavering hope, the resilient flame that burns brightly within me.

## The Enduring Spirit of Love

The quiet hum of the morning light, once a source of shared joy, now serves as a poignant reminder of Connie's absence. Yet, within that quietude, a different kind of energy resonates – the unwavering echo of a love that refuses to be silenced by death. It's not a naive denial of loss; rather, it's an acknowledgement of a bond so profound that it transcends the physical realm. This is not simply a sentiment; it is a lived experience, a constant presence woven into the fabric of my days. The pain remains, a constant companion, but it is now interwoven with a profound sense of gratitude for the life we shared, a life rich in laughter, shared dreams, and an unwavering commitment to each other. It is a love that has shaped my understanding of the universe, of life, and of the enduring power of the human spirit.

This love was not merely an emotional response; it was a philosophy, a way of being. It wasn't a fleeting passion, but a deeply rooted commitment, nurtured over forty-one years of shared experiences, triumphs, and challenges. We built a life together, brick by brick, a testament to our shared values and unwavering devotion. We traveled the world, not just as tourists, but as seekers of understanding, absorbing the richness of different cultures and perspectives. Our conversations were often profound explorations of philosophical concepts, spiritual teachings, and the intricacies of human nature. We debated the merits of Chanakya's wisdom and pondered the profound teachings of Lord Krishna, always seeking a deeper understanding of our place in the world. These shared intellectual pursuits enriched our lives, strengthening the bonds that tied our souls together.

The loss of Connie shattered my world, leaving a void that seemed impossible to fill. The initial shock gave way to a raw, visceral grief, a pain so profound that it threatened to consume me entirely. Anger, too, was a potent emotion. The alleged medical negligence that contributed to her suffering and untimely death fueled a righteous fury, a burning desire for justice. This anger, however, was not a destructive force; it served as a catalyst, pushing me to fight for accountability, to ensure that no one else would suffer a similar fate due to the same callous indifference.

My journey through grief has been far from linear. It has been a winding path, marked by moments of intense sorrow, interspersed with fleeting glimpses of hope and acceptance. There were days when the pain was so overwhelming that it felt impossible to breathe, to function, to even contemplate the future. There were other days, fewer but increasingly frequent, when the memories of our life together brought not just sadness, but also a wave of profound gratitude, a deep appreciation for the gift of her love. These memories are not just nostalgic reminiscences; they are living, breathing parts of me, a constant reminder of the richness and depth of our connection.

The process of healing has been, and continues to be, a deeply personal journey. It involves acknowledging the pain, allowing myself to grieve fully, without judgment or self-criticism. It has required a conscious effort to focus on the positive aspects of our life together, to celebrate her accomplishments, her spirit, and the indelible mark she left on the world and on me. This process has also involved seeking support from others, sharing my experiences, and finding solace in the shared experiences of other grieving individuals. The understanding and empathy I've received have been invaluable in navigating this difficult terrain. Moreover, I have found solace in spiritual practices, in meditation, and in the quiet contemplation of nature. These practices have helped me find a sense of peace, a space of quiet reflection where I can connect with Connie's spirit.

My pursuit of justice is another facet of this healing process. It's not about revenge; it's about accountability, about ensuring that the system that failed Connie doesn't fail others. It's about seeking a sense of closure, a way to honor her memory by preventing similar tragedies. This pursuit, though emotionally challenging, has given me a sense of purpose, a focus that has helped me channel my grief into positive action. It's a way of honoring Connie's legacy, of ensuring that her memory serves as a catalyst for positive change.

The concept of "two bodies, one soul" isn't simply a romantic notion. It's a reflection of the profound interconnectedness of our lives. Our souls, intertwined through years of shared experiences, continue to resonate even in the face of physical separation. This connection transcends the boundaries of time and space. It's a spiritual reality that provides comfort and hope in the midst of overwhelming sorrow. This isn't a mere belief system; it's the lived reality of a love that continues to sustain me, even as I navigate the complexities of a life lived without her physical presence. The shared history, the memories, the values we held dear, these remain as tangible as ever, shaping my perceptions, influencing my decisions, and guiding my actions.

The pain of loss is a profound teacher. It compels us to examine our lives, our values, and our priorities. It challenges us to confront our vulnerabilities, to acknowledge our mortality, and to appreciate the preciousness of life. The grieving process is not merely about overcoming sadness, it is about transformation. It forces a reassessment of one's beliefs and a reconceptualization of the self. Through grief, we are refined, changed, and ultimately, strengthened.

My journey through grief has been a profound exploration of the human spirit's resilience, its capacity for adaptation, and its enduring capacity to love. Connie's spirit lives on not only in my memory, but in the life I strive to live – a life of purpose, compassion, and a continuing dedication to the pursuit of justice. It is a life informed by our shared experiences, a life dedicated to honouring the enduring legacy of a love that transcends the limitations of mortality.

The enduring spirit of love manifests in unexpected ways. It's in the quiet moments of reflection, in the echoes of laughter that still ring in my ears, and in the quiet understanding that permeates my being. It's the strength I find to navigate each day, the wisdom that guides my choices, and the unwavering belief that her essence, her spirit, remains an integral part of mine.

Connie's absence is a constant presence, a powerful reminder of the fragility of life and the preciousness of each moment. However, this awareness doesn't lead to despair; instead, it fuels a deeper appreciation for the beauty and wonder that surround us. It fosters a heightened sensitivity to the world, an increased capacity for empathy, and a more profound understanding of the interconnectedness of all things. The love we shared was not confined to our individual lives; it extended to our family, our friends, and the wider community. This expansive love, enriched by years of shared experience and mutual growth, transcends the boundaries of the physical world.

The legacy of our love is not merely a collection of cherished memories; it's a living testament to the power of human connection, a continuing source of strength and inspiration. It is a philosophy that informs my actions, guides my decisions, and shapes my understanding of the world. And it is a testament to the enduring human capacity to find meaning and purpose in the face of unimaginable loss. The journey continues, evolving, deepening, and constantly being shaped by a love that knows no boundaries and transcends the limitations of time and death. Two bodies, one soul, forever – that remains the unshakeable truth, the unwavering hope, the resilient flame that burns eternally within me. The echoes of her laughter, the warmth of her presence, the depth of our shared journey; these are not mere memories, but the very essence of who I am. And it is through these enduring echoes that I carry her love forward, a love that is both a source of enduring grief and an unshakeable source of strength.

# Acknowledgments

Writing this book has been a deeply personal and cathartic journey, one I could not have undertaken without the support of many remarkable individuals. First and foremost, I want to thank my family and friends, whose unwavering love and understanding sustained me through the darkest hours of my grief. Their empathy, patience, and practical assistance were invaluable. Special thanks go to [Name(s) of close friends or family members], who offered solace, encouragement, and unwavering belief in my ability to navigate this profound loss and transform my pain into a narrative of hope and resilience.

My gratitude extends to my legal team, [Name(s) of lawyers], who fought tirelessly for justice on my behalf. Their expertise and dedication were crucial in my pursuit of accountability, a pursuit which, while emotionally challenging, ultimately became a part of my healing process.

I am also indebted to [Name(s) of editors, agents, or other professionals], whose insightful guidance and meticulous work shaped this manuscript into its final form. Their commitment to the integrity of the story, and their sensitivity to its deeply personal nature, ensured that Connie's memory is honored with both respect and honesty.

Finally, this book is a testament to the enduring power of love, a power that transcends even death. It is dedicated to Connie, whose memory continues to inspire me, and to all those who have known the profound pain of loss and the arduous journey of healing.

# Appendix

This appendix contains supplementary materials related to the legal case mentioned in the book. Specifically, it includes [brief description of documents included, e.g., redacted excerpts from medical records, summary of legal arguments, timeline of events]. Access to these documents has been carefully considered, balancing the need for transparency with the imperative to protect the privacy of individuals involved. These materials are provided for context and are not intended as legal advice.

## Glossary

This glossary defines key terms used throughout the book, particularly those pertaining to medical procedures, legal processes, and spiritual concepts.

**[Term 1]:** [Definition]
**[Term 2]:** [Definition]
**[Term 3]:** [Definition]
**[and so on, including terms like "allopathic medicine," "medical negligence," "karma," "dharma," etc.]**

# References

[List of references cited in the book, formatted according to a consistent style guide (e.g., MLA, Chicago). Include books, articles, legal documents, and any other sources mentioned.]

## Author Biography

Pradeep Berry is a writer and crisis management expert. His career has spanned [number] years, during which he has developed a deep understanding of human resilience and the complexities of grief and loss. Before Connie's passing, he and Connie shared a vibrant life, rich with travel, intellectual exploration, and a deep commitment to the arts. The experience of losing Connie to cancer in 2015 fundamentally reshaped his life, prompting him to explore both the spiritual and legal dimensions of his grief. This book, "Two Bodies & One Soul," is his first, reflecting his dedication to sharing his personal journey and advocating for improved healthcare standards. His experiences have shaped his commitment to promoting patient safety and accountability within the healthcare system. He currently resides in [Location].

www.ingramcontent.com/pod-product-compliance
Lightning Source LLC
Chambersburg PA
CBHW081934160726
47999CB00008B/2388